Conversation

*An Ex-SPY's Guide to Master
the Art of Mind Control Through
Powerful Persuasion Techniques &
Conversational Tactics for Ultimate
Influence in Any Situation*

JAMES DAUGHERTY

TABLE OF CONTENTS

INTRODUCTION

"If you just communicate, you can get by. But if you communicate skillfully, you can work miracles"

(Jim Rohn)

Communication is one of the most important aspects of everyday life. A person will generally be able to get so much more out of his or her day just by developing and enhancing their communication skills.

As a spy, I was required to use such skills to enter and exit many types of situations. These were the type of interactions that would be common in everyday life, general contact making and rapport building for the most part, however some did venture towards high-pressure stakes from time to time. One important tool that I extensively used during such situations was persuasion. Persuasion is a subtle, elegant art and psychological tactic that one can covertly implement to gain high levels of influence over others when done correctly.

Not to be confused with manipulation and deception, persuasion is a technique that should naturally alter people's feelings and thoughts and gets them to come round to your way of thinking. It's a simple technique that can help you when chasing after your desires and goals as it will smooth the interactions you have big and small that will ultimately have others batting for your success. The good news is, that like every psychological technique I describe in this book and others, high level persuasion proficiency is possible to learn, adopt and implement with the correct training and application. Believe me, it's a skill set that you really want as it's the one thing that will allow you to garner the most (and more importantly) the correct influence in any situation.

This book has been crafted to educate you on the many aspects of persuasion and how you can implement them in your daily life. As an ex-spy who was exposed to all types of scenarios, I have compiled this book based on my personal experiences from both my time and training with the FBI and also the trials and tribulations I faced whilst in the field as a CIA operative.

As most of us know, the human mind can be easy to influence but takes a certain knack to persuade others in the right way in order to get them to listen to you.

My job scope required me to extensively work on people's minds from the inside in order to get them to do things for me on the outside. I made use of certain techniques that I will lay out in the following chapters. But you must understand that you need not be a spy to follow these strategies. They are universal and can be applied in all walks of life. You will find that you will naturally be doing many of these things already, especially if you are a more empathetic and social person. But it's still a good idea to pin point exactly what you are doing right, why that it's working and to learn new skills that will push you to improve even further.

Human behavior is pretty much the most predictable thing on the planet. If you know these patterns on a personal level and on a wider societal level, then you can start play the game of influence and persuasion with a great deal of success.

But before that, here is a little background into my life and why I'm a useful person to listen to when it comes to persuasion.

My Back Story

As with all of the subjects I have previously written on, you may be thinking, "Who is this guy that he is such an expert in persuasion? Why should I listen to him?" That's an important question, so here is what you need to know about me.

Firstly, I want you to think about everything you have ever learned about spies from the movies. Think about action-packed scenes, dangerous surveillance, and anything else you have learned from Hollywood. Now, take these preconceived notions and toss them out the window. Real spy work is not indiscriminate violence and high speed chases. Real spy work is usually done from afar; it's about getting things done with minimal fuss and without provocation. It's quiet and unassuming data gathering for the most part.

You'd also be surprised to find that spy work isn't necessarily gadgets and glzmos that do your work for you Most of the time, it comes down to human psychological skills and the ability to improvise in any situation. And these skills can be developed and learned with a little practice.

I have to skip over some of the more specific details, as almost everything I have done over the past two decades is classified. Real names will be omitted as I detail some of my jobs and experiences around the world for the same reason.

I got my start in 1994 working a desk job for the FBI in my home state of Virginia. About a decade into my stint with them, my parents died in a car accident in our home town whilst sliding on an icy road into oncoming traffic one winter. Since it was my ties to my family that had kept me at home all these years, I decided to become a field agent as I figured I'd get to see a fair deal more than I currently was paper pushing behind a desk in Richmond. The transition wasn't as smooth as I'd anticipated. But a little under nine months after undertaking the training, I was a fully fledged Special Agent in the FBI. It took me all across the country, initially shadowing more experienced agents on white collar fraud cases but I soon graduated onto much more interesting work.

I have to confess that I did not know how good I would be at first. Everything that I had done in life up to this point though, I had succeeded at. From top grades in high school to the football scholarship at Florida State that I used to study forensics and psychology, I had succeeded in pretty much everything I'd tried. Regardless of why, I was good.

The FBI took note of this as they put me on more dangerous assignments as an undercover agent. I infiltrated criminal organizations and helped to take down illegal rackets of all descriptions. Sex, drugs, you name it. Eventually, I ended up on a case with another agent, an American spy. It was through him that I met my latest employer.

So, why am I an expert in persuasion? I have since left the CIA, but after many years working for them as a spy I had acquired a number unique skill sets, counterintelligence, hand-to-hand combat, lock picking, body language analysis just to name a few. However, the ability to persuade people successfully in a range of situations was a big a part of my day-to-day for obvious reasons.

In my professional career I was both formally trained in persuasion techniques during my years with the FBI and then with a more hands on experience in the field as a CIA intelligence operative. This started with run of the mill street level dealings getting gangsters and crooks on my side whilst undercover but advanced to some of the highest level decision making with government officials and political players from all around the world, the types of things that really make a difference to how the world works today.

So now that you know my qualifications and what I bring to the table, let's dive in. The following chapters will teach you everything that you need to become proficient in persuasion, especially in those critical moments that matter most. Don't worry, I will provide plenty of stories about my work in the field (as well as real life scenarios that could apply to you) along the way to keep things interesting. But ultimately provide you with the tools and knowledge on how to persuade your way to a better outcome in any situation.

PART 1

UNDERSTANDING THE THEORY OF PERSUASION TECHNIQUES AND WHEN TO USE THEM

CHAPTER 1

CIALDINI'S 6 "WEAPONS" OF INFLUENCE EXPLAINED

"Influence is the compass, persuasion is the map"

(Joseph Wong)

Now unless you have completely cut yourself off from the outside world and live under a rock, you will not be able to escape influence. Persuasion is prevalent in every walk of life, be it college, work or even in the supermarket. People will try to influence you in one way or another.

As a matter of fact, you can successfully identify any situation where you are being influenced and stop it from affecting you. In this segment, we will look at the basics of persuasion and catch up on some of its important aspects.

Persuasion is a natural human tendency. Majorities of people get influenced easily and give into what someone else has to say to them. If you wish to use persuasion to your advantage and learn how to go about it, then here are basic principles to bear in mind.

Now whilst I have had plenty of experience using persuasion in intense real life situations, there are others who have academically studied the principles in greater depth. One of those is professor of psychology, Robert Cialdini. According to Cialdini there are 6 major principles or "weapons" of persuasion. They are written with a more commercial context in mind, for selling and the advertising industry. But they can equally be applied to the psychology of human behavior on an interpersonal level. I must say that I agree that they all play a part in successful persuasion at one time or another and they definitely serve as a good basis to explore the basic principles before I head into my rather more gritty advice on the matter. But firstly here is my take on them.

Reciprocity

The first principle of persuasion is reciprocity. It is based on the theory that when you offer something to someone, they will feel indebted and have an urge to reciprocate it back. Humans seem innately wired to feel this way and act like this from an evolutionary stand point; it appears that compassion for another person, especially when they have performed a kind act in your favor is hard not to reciprocate.

Counter to the "all for themselves" mentality painted by many historians, early human civilization had to be predicated largely on cooperation and community to survive and thrive. But this principle is still applicable to almost every situation in life today. Whilst I certainly used this principle to a more definite and intentional ends throughout the years, it does not mean you have to view it like that. It can sometimes seem to be the most manipulative principle if you look at it in the wrong way. It is more advisable to cultivate a giving attitude in general and let this law play out naturally. I don't want to get into the metaphysical claims about getting back a certain factor more than you give out to the world as I'm not some esoteric self help guru, but there is certainly some truth to it. But here are some things to do in order to use it to your advantage if you so choose.

- Always make the first move. You must offer something first in order to make the other person feel indebted to you.

- Next, offer them something they can only get from you where possible. If you give them something exclusive then it will further work in your favor.

- Personalize what you give so that they know who it came from. Make it special for them so that they internalize the event more effectively.

Following these simple steps will help you persuade a person in some future interaction down the line. If you do these things enough and in the right way you shouldn't actually have to do much persuading at all, as the person will naturally jump at the chance to help you out to return the favor.

There have been experiments conducted in American restaurants where it was found that the more attention and generosity the waiter showcased, the higher he was tipped by customers. They would give the customers a toffee and receive an 18% tip. When they increased it to 2 toffees, they received a 21% tip in return. So the moral of the story is give out a lot of toffees, you never know what might come back.

Commitment & Consistency

It is human nature to settle for whatever has already been tried and tested in their mind. They will have a mental image of who they are and how things should be. I always think back to the analogy within the movie "The Matrix" when describing this principle to people where Laurence Fishburne's character Morpheus is explaining to Neo the concept of his 'residual self image', that his perception of himself within the matrix is merely a projection, a digital image of his mental self. This is true for people in everyday life too; they really want to remain consistent with what their values and beliefs align with and who they think they really are.

Most people will not be up for experimenting and act in a way they have always done so in the past. So to influence someone through this principle, you have to first get them to commit to something. It might seem a little tough to do so at first, as it requires a certain commitment on your part too, but following a few simple rules can help you with it. The following steps will help you in persuading a person through the consistency and commitment principle.

- Get the person to start small so that they can manage the change before they integrate it with their personality and get hooked on the habit.

- Get them to accept something publically so they will feel the urge to stick with it and obligated to see it through.

- Reward the person for sticking to the course. Giving away rewards can help with strengthening a person's interest in whatever you are trying to get them to go along with.

Like every technique I describe in this book and others, consistency is always the key to its eventual success and the situation is no different here.

Social Proof

This principle is another human tendency and one in which we tend to place a high amount of stock and trust in other people and their opinions on things we haven't tried for ourselves. This is especially relevant if the opinion is coming from a perceived/credible expert or a close friend. Nobody has the time to try everything in life so we naturally have to rely on others and take cues from them on experiences we haven't yet had. I'm sure you are drawn to products and services that are endorsed by experts just because you think they know what they are saying or equate a person's fame and celebrity with validity for the product, which is a very common marketing tactic every big company employs. The same extends to other people who will take to something if another trustworthy person endorses it. Humans are pattern seekers by nature and we are continually looking to connect the dots of evidence around us and take shortcuts to the answers. Here is a closer look at some of the aspects of this theory.

- The first step will be to obtain credible support from experts in the field. This will work like a charm, as people will take to it instantly.

- As I mentioned above, most people like it if their favorite celebrity endorses a product. They will take a liking to it especially if the celebrity claims to use the product himself or herself.

- People prefer it if others like them are also indulging in the similar behavior. They will take to it if they find that someone else likes them doing it.

- Apart from individuals, people are also more comfortable when larger parts of the population approve of their behavior. A person is more likely to buy or do something if their friends and family members approve of it; people just love following the crowd as it makes them feel safe and accepted.

In a study conducted in 1935, many subjects were placed in a dark room with a small dot of light in the distance. The subjects were asked to observe the dot and guess how many times it moved. Each of the participants had a different answer they gave when initially asked. However when all of them were assembled in one room and had time to discuss the outcome and then asked the same question they all agreed on just one unanimous answer that was in fact much different from what they had originally guessed. These types of studies have been conducted for over a hundred years and even before Cialdini wrote about them within the 1980's.

Today the internet is awash with social proof examples especially when it comes to social media and online advertising. Companies are desperate to garner engagement, likes and shares of their carefully integrated ads, they even pay 'influencers' with large followings thousands of dollars to promote their products for the exact same reason.

Likeability

We all know that we are generally attracted to a certain set of people that we consider likable. This extends to friends and family members alike. So in order to get others to like you and in turn be open to persuasion by you, you must first transition into a friend or acquaintance. The basic premise of this book and even "Negotiation: An Ex-SPY's guide" in really making the principles work, is to create an empathetic environment first. This ties in closely with the reciprocity principle and here are some basic steps to follow for the same result.

- The first step will be the attraction phase. You will have to give a person something that they will be instantly drawn to.

- Make it relatable. People will be drawn to you if you are in turn relatable to them. You will find it easier to influence someone if they consider you their friend.

- It will be vital to communicate as a friend. You will have to make use of good communication skills to get into their good books.

- Make it look like you are in the same group as them and fighting for the same causes. This will help increase rapport.

Authority

If you wish to influence someone then you must dress and act the part. This means that you wear clothes and accessories that help you look like you are in command. Although this might seem quite superficial, it will only help you achieve your end goal. Here are some of the criteria to bear in mind.

- Wear clothes that are befitting of people's perception of authoritative figures within their life.

- Communicate to them in a direct commanding fashion.

- Make sure you learn the language and lexicon of the experts in that field. Talk how they talk.

There are many studies that have also confirmed this authority principle and none more so than the famous Milgram obedience experiments. These studies were conducted at Yale University by psychologist Stanley Milgram in 1963, where an experimenter instructed a teacher to ask questions to a learner (actor). The teacher was instructed to pass increasingly greater electric shocks to the learner if he failed to answer a question correctly. The learner was instructed to give away wrong answers and act like he was in pain when the fake shock was administered.

The researchers were surprised to find that the teacher would continue to pass the electric shock to the learner, sometimes with even the highest voltage just because the experimenter would ask him to despite not hearing a response from the learner, who was now asked to be silent. This illustrated that the teacher would simply follow instructions from the experimenter even we they believed they were delivering a potentially lethal shock just because someone of authority was telling them to do so.

The findings of these experiments were later cited at many German Nazi war criminal hearings taking into consideration that the thousands of Germans complicit in the concentration camps of the holocaust were simply following orders from extremely authoritative figures.

Scarcity

The last "weapon" of influence of the 6 is the principle of scarcity. Human beings like exclusivity and are drawn to things that they will not find anywhere else. By making something exclusive you will have the chance to enhance its value. They are also fearful when something they desire starts to disappear. It's your classic supply and demand principle, if something is abundant than it will have a perceived lower value and be cheap, if it is rare then it will have high value and be expensive.

This works for products and human beings in exactly the same way. Here are some aspects to bear in mind.

- Always imply that whatever you are offering (whether it is something physical or information) is not available anywhere else.

- Try to implement a countdown timer on whatever you are offering so there is a clear indication of when it will disappear.

- Never go back on the original stipulations I mentioned above. It's critical to show people that what you offered them was indeed genuinely scarce to ensure the effectiveness of this method in future instances.

I have seen these types of tactics employed all over the world. From street level narcotics dealers driving up the price of their product through some sort of engineered shortage, to entire populations hoarding gas and food supplies on warnings of bad weather. Anything that is in high demand which is seen to be getting increasingly more difficult to acquire will become more valuable. As I mentioned, criminals and politicians use this tactic all of the time and you should too when it comes to persuasion in your everyday dealings.

CHAPTER 2

CLASSIC PSYCHOLOGICAL MOTIVATORS

Before we get into anymore specific tactics of persuasion, it is critical to back up a bit to understand the base psychological needs and motivators of other humans if you intend to persuade them in anyway. Once you understand what concerns people and their patterns of interest, it's much easier to get them to your way of thinking as you can essentially align yourself with what they are striving for and go along with the flow.

Human beings actually only require a few basic elements in order to survive. Once those physiological needs are fulfilled they then turn to psychological motivators in order to go after more advanced needs. This is where I'll spend the majority of this book, exploring the mental techniques involved in persuasion. But firstly, in this chapter, we will look at both of these physical and mental aspects in detail.

According to Abraham Maslow and his pyramid or hierarchy of needs, all human beings have 5 types of needs namely physiological needs, safety needs, social needs, self-acceptance and self- actualization. Physiological needs are basic needs. Basic needs refer to the absolute essential requirements a person needs to survive which include food, shelter and clothing. Having these things in place are obviously the base essentials a person needs to function in everyday life. Only once these things are satisfied can a person turn their energy towards attaining their ambitions and self-actualization goals. These ambitions of course vary from person to person and depend entirely on what a person envisions for themselves. The means to attain them will also vary. But in general they will all be categorized in much the same way

Here is a breakdown of the essentials as discussed by Maslow.

Basic Needs

Food, Warmth, Shelter

These are basic physiological and biological needs we simple have to attain first and foremost before any thought of betterment can be entertained. This is where we spent much of our early evolution as a species, long grinding progress where the majority of our time was spent hunting and foraging for food, building fires to stay warm and finding shelter for somewhere to sleep. I imagine every person reading this will have these things covered but sadly there is still an element of this today, people living in stark poverty and homelessness throughout the world. I have traveled to countless countries on every continent and its prevalence especially in developing nations is still much higher than it should be considering the wealth that is generated elsewhere.

Security, Safety

Along the same lines as the above, there are a few more basic elements a human being needs to fulfill before they can really pursue any proper lifestyle improvements. They require a safe and secure environment, protection from the outside elements within a sturdy and secure apartment building or house. They need to be free of the fear of violence and confident in the law and order systems that surround them. Only then can they start to move to the next level of needs.

Psychological Needs

Acceptance, Sense of Belonging

All human beings crave a sense of acceptance. We are social animals and crave belonging to a group. People put in efforts to socialize as it serves as a motivation to feel accepted. Other people's opinions matter to them, thereby making it necessary to remain within social circles. The common evolutionary thinking is that we developed the fast majority of our social etiquette and norms when we used to live in small groups of 100-150 people on the African savannas when it was imperative to integrate harmoniously because being outcast meant almost certain death.

When a person has the base physiological requirements met, they will then start to look for this acceptance, friendships, trust and intimacy to satisfy this sense for belonging.

Self Esteem, Prestige, Accomplishment

Once the base psychological needs are met it's then time to start to explore an even greater level mental fulfillment. These elements are more closely concerned with climbing the social pecking order to some extent. Initially to find a greater sense of confidence and self esteem for oneself before looking to achieve more independence, self-respect and ultimately a higher level of prestige and status within society as a result.

Self-Fulfillment Needs

Self-Actualization, Creativity, Full Potential

Then only after fully satisfying the base physiological and psychological needs beneath it in the pyramid can a person finally move onto the last stage of requirements which is the self-fulfillment needs. This is where everybody should be in order to lead a totally fulfilling life, when everything else is taken care of in terms of a security and prosperity standpoint. This place is as much about giving back then anything.

A person is now free to fully explore what they believe to be their true purpose in life and spend as much time as they wish developing their creative tendencies. This level is all about peak experiences and personal growth. From what I see in the world, only a handful of people relatively speaking currently reach this stage. The rest are making the upward struggle somewhere in the middle of this pyramid of needs.

Neuroscience of Motivation

I explain this in greater detail with "Self-Discipline: An Ex-SPY's Guide" but the neurobiological roots of the human motivation behavior originate in the basal ganglia and dopaminergic pathways in the brain. Seeking style behavior will activate and release a cascade of the dopaminergic drugs such as the pleasure hormone dopamine in anticipation of a reward. This is what you are intending to trigger during the persuasion process.

In more general terms, motivation is a theoretical construct scientists use to explain human behavior, a motive that will prompt a person to act in a certain way. It is also a directional process either directed toward positive stimuli or away from negative ones. In layman's terms that really just means that humans are either trying to attain something they like (wealth, health, status) or trying to avoid and escape something they do not (hard work, poverty, discomfort). In my experience of witnessing thousands of people from different countries and cultures around the world, it is almost always and universally the latter that drives people for the most part. Here's quick tip, one very easy way to motivate and persuade a person to do anything is to offer them a solution to a problem that is causing them discomfort or something they are desperately trying to avoid.

And remember that humans are not the rational beings they were once thought. Recent research has severely undermined the "Perfect Rationality" suppositions within economics and game theory where a person is thought to act in a way to maximize utility. But rather "Bounded Rationality" is now the order of the day which takes into consideration the large cognitive limitations humans possess when it comes to assessing value and time limitations of opportunities in front of them. It is up to you to explore, expose and play on these limitation tendencies in thinking to better play the persuasion game.

There are a few other noteworthy factors worth mentioning and to take into consideration when assessing a person's psychological motivations which all can be played on to increase persuasive success. These are additional human behaviors that make up a person's mental makeup such as curiosity, honor, idealism, power, romance and vengeance. So see when you can spot each one and when you may be able to use this urge in someone to your advantage.

So in summarizing this chapter, it is a cliché to say that all humans are essentially the same, but in reality it is not far from the truth. To say that human behavior is one of the most, if not the most predictable thing on the planet and I would certainly not disagree. People are basically very similar in their needs and desires. They differ only very slightly due to upbringing and culture but in a base sense, as described by Maslow's physiological and psychological needs pyramid, they are indistinguishable.

It really is just about assessing where a person is regarding their level of development on their way through the pyramid. If you can more closely relate to what they are going through and what is concerning and dominating their thinking, you can much more likely suggest things that they will be open to and resonate with, making them much easier to persuade in the process.

CHAPTER 3

THE DIFFERENT TYPES OF PERSUASION TECHNIQUES

In the opening chapter to this book, we looked at Robert Cialdini's 6 basic principles of influencing people. They can be extremely powerful when used to good effect.

Apart from those ones however, there are certain other ways in which people can influence others. As a spy, I had to make use of a diverse set of tactics as although most people are generally the same, they will in fact respond to a slightly different approach depending on the situation at hand.

Firstly I think it's a good idea to state exactly what persuasion is. It's simply the process or action taken by a person or group of people when they cause something to change. This will be in relation to another human being and something that changes their inner mental systems (attitudes, values & beliefs) or their external behavior patterns (actions & habits). The act of persuasion may also create something new within the person or may just modify something that already exists in their mind.

In my experience both types of persuasion has its problems and obstacles, getting somebody to do something completely new can be challenging as they have no prior reference point for it and will naturally be cautious or even dubious about trying it. Similarly getting a person to change or modify an existing thought pattern or behavior can be equally as tough as they are already set in their ways. Remember humans are pattern seekers by nature and are looking to connect the dots and find evidence to back up what they already believe as it's easier than re-thinking the whole thing. It's your job to go along with these patterns of thought when you can but disrupt, break up and redirect them when you cannot (pointers on this to come).

In terms of the process, persuasion is usually comprised of three parts:

1. The communicator or source of persuasion

2. The actual persuasive nature of the appeal

3. The target person/audience of the appeal

All three elements need to be taken into account before attempting any high level persuasions. It's good practice to look around you in your daily life and watch out for when these subtle (and sometimes overt) persuasions are happening. It's good training for when you want to employ similar tactics yourself or just as importantly to make sure you are not on the end of something you do not want to be.

The 3 Aristotelian Appeals

"Character may almost be called the most effective means of persuasion"

(Aristotle)

The ancient Greek philosopher Aristotle is perhaps the most famous arguer and persuader of all time. He believed that there were generally three ways a person could approach things when they indented to persuade and change the opinion of another person.

Ethos

The first of these appeals he described is Ethos, which focuses on attributes such as character, integrity and trust. It focuses on the reputation of a person, what they may have done in the past and what others speak about them today. Reputations can be a very important thing to protect especially for politicians in high office or anybody in the public eye who wants to maintain any degree of influence over others. It's OK to show character, that you are a human being just like everybody else and even have some flaws. The trick is to ensure that they are small enough or irrelevant enough for the target audience not to care too much about, but large enough to show you as a person of good values and virtues.

Lastly, Aristotle explains how credibility can play a large factor in someone's persuasive power. Much like Cialdini's modern principle of social proof, people will more likely believe something that is coming from a perceived expert in that field. So make sure you cultivate this impression where you can through strong affirmative communication and gestures.

Pathos

Pathos is a quality that is more concerned with evoking the emotions of the listener, seeking in some way to excite them or arouse interest in what you are saying. This can most effectively be done through storytelling and referencing situations where injustices may have occurred or innocent people adversely affected. In turn you may use Ethos to condemn such action and describe your own high values and beliefs about the matter.

Linguistics also plays a big role when it comes to the Pathos appeal as language is such an effective tool for eliciting emotional responses. A good speaker and orator will always plan their words carefully by using hot and cold keywords to either amplify (intentional, anger, fire) or subdue a situation (careful, smooth, irrelevant). The next time you are watching a politician in a parliamentary debate or taking questions from the press, watch how they inflate or downplay whatever they are referring to depending on the spin they want to put on it. It was my job to coach this into certain foreign leaders who weren't quite ready for release yet.

Logos

The final approach is Logos which is actually an appeal to logic, rational explanation and evidence towards the argument at hand. As well as being a philosopher, Aristotle was also a prominent scientist of his time and believed highly in the use of empirical evidence to prove a point. He tried to encourage this as much as possible within law making and common discourse alike. The courts were especially interesting to him as all three appeals could come into play. Pathos being evoked when somebody is trying to put a positive or negative spin on a statement, Ethos to establish a witness's credibility and finally Logos to provide the evidence.

So after reviewing some of the over arching persuasion principles, it's now time to delve into some of the specific strategies that you can apply in everyday discourse which also helped me carve out useful relationships in the field.

Persuasion is both an art and a science. It is a science because you must first learn the high level skills and principles required to persuade someone effectively. It is an art to know exactly when to employ the strategies for the best results. In a day, most of us find ourselves in many types of persuasive scenarios. So go over the following techniques and see how best you can apply them to your situation.

Start Small (Foot in the door)

The first principle is just like what it sounds, before asking anybody for any large favor or request, you initially ask for a smaller one first. By doing so, the person will develop a helpful mindset towards you. Once the small task is fulfilled, they will commit to fulfilling any larger task at some point in the future. It will also be easier for you to approach someone with a smaller task compared to asking for something bigger and more cumbersome, so that's where you should start.

Going about it systematically can help with getting the favor approved. This technique was tested out in 1966, when two Stanford professors divided 156 women into 4 groups. They asked the first 3 groups various simple questions about their kitchen. A week later, they asked the same women to catalog their kitchen products, no quick or easy task for these individuals. The first three groups showed a 52.8% success rate in cataloguing the products while the fourth group showed only a success rate of just 22.2%. This shows that asking for a smaller task before the bigger one can help increase chances of getting it done.

This is actually the main premise of a confidence trick that con artists often employ. They will initially ask for a small amount of money, a hundred dollars or so to bet on a certain stock on your behalf due to some "insider" knowledge. They will obviously return a win for the mark often doubling or tripling the initial stakes. They will then go back to the mark some weeks later to ask them to invest a little more, this time a few hundred dollars and turn around a similar result. This will escalate until enough trust is built within the relationship when the con artist will now offer the mark the big prize, the real inside bet that will make them millions. So the mark gladly hands over any winnings they've accumulated thus far and usually their entire savings to boot. However unsurprisingly they never usually see the con artist or their money ever again…

Now as I mentioned in the opening remarks to this book, the persuasion techniques I describe in these chapters are not intended to be underhand or manipulative to somebody else's detriment. But rather subtle persuasion tactics designed to nudge people in the right direction. But the con artist analogy very clearly illustrates a point on this one.

Anchoring

I touched on this within "Negotiation; An-Ex SPY's Guide". Anchoring refers to a technique where a person uses a benchmark to influence another person. This technique is widely used in many circumstances as it can be very efficient in garnering a positive result. Say for example you are trying to sell a ballpoint pen that is priced at $10. The customer negotiates it to $8. The customer will walk away happy knowing that a product's price was reduced to suit his or her need but in actuality, the price of the pen was increased just that morning from $6 to $10. So in effect, you manage to make a profit on the product and satisfy the customer at the same time, all by initially anchoring the price at a higher point to begin with.

This theory was tested by a group of economists who offered students 3 annual subscription selections to pick from when signing up for a popular magazine. The first option was to choose a web only version for just $59, the second was to choose the printed option for $125 and the third was to choose web and print for $125. 16 students ended up choosing the first option while 84 chose the third (nobody went for the second option). After a few days time, the second option was actually eliminated. It was interesting to note that the vast majority of the students who choose the third option stuck with it as the second option was a mere decoy placed to enhance the value of the third option. It worked as an anchor for students to compare with the third option.

Reversal Tagging

Reversal tagging is a simple and subtle sentence phrasing trick that can be used to gain compliance or agreement from somebody in general. It is a method that uses two opposing structures to a sentence, the first component being an affirmative statement and second being a tag question. The premise here is to make the initial statement to open the line of questioning but add the tag question to give the person a binary choice when answering. That way you can reframe whatever response they give to make it sound as if they are agreeing with you all along.

You might say to your spouse "You like this house, don't you?" They might reply "Yes, I like this place" to which your respond "As I thought, you like this place." However if you had gotten the opposite response i.e. "You like this house, don't you?" to which they replied "No, I don't like this place" you simply say "As I thought, you don't like this place."

Statements like this are designed to have a negative reversal element to them, such as "he did call you, didn't he?" If done correctly the structure of the statement should hide the command in the form of a rhetorical question, by first telling the person what they should be thinking but inserting the question that offers a level of disagreement but also implying that this is not wanted (as it would be contradictory towards the already made assertion).

The key to this working is ensuring that the first statement is a strong one as it will be the main persuasive component to the principle. "She's correct, isn't she?" is different from "She's not correct, is she?" These are both technically reversals but the first is much more affirmative and effective then the second. Also be careful not to take too long of a pause in between the two components of the statement or have a very obvious rising tone to the tag question "David's happy.... isn't he?" This may invoke confusion and suspicion or even contention of the point. So make sure it's it flows well and reasonably neutral in its intonation.

This technique can also be used when persuading a person to actually take action on something as opposed to simply agreeing with you. It's the same principle and structure but this time you state the negative first and take a longer pause before the tag question "You aren't able to do that.... are you?" If you imply to a person that they cannot do something it will evoke a reactive response to prove you wrong, you still add the reversal tag question to soften the statement. This is much like the principle of reverse psychology that I will explain in greater detail next.

Reverse Psychology

This one should be familiar with just about everyone as it is a common psychological tactic used when trying to get another person to take an action. However it can seem obvious and clichéd if not performed in the correct and subtle manner. It is essentially getting somebody to do something by initially suggesting that they do the opposite. It is also more effective if the suggestion evokes an emotional response as they are less likely to think it through rationally and just react. This is especially true when you are suggesting they cannot do something they are stating themselves (but you also want them to do) i.e. "I could finish this all today if wanted too" to which you reply "I'm sure you could, but you usually work to slowly..." They will more than likely do it to prove you wrong.

"Elegant persuasion is when the other person thought
it was their idea"

(Marshall Sylver)

This principle is more likely to work with individuals who need to be in control more often than not, rebellious types like teenage children who naturally want to do the opposite to what their parents are telling them. It's actually termed "Reactance theory" and describes a scenario where a person feels like they have lost control and attempts to grab it back by doing the opposite of what they are asked, even if it is not in their best interest.

As I mentioned above, a reverse psychology statement needs to be done correctly to avoid detection as it is so common. Make sure you cloak the statement as much as possible and use a neutral or even dismissive tone to imply that you are indifferent to their response.

Cognitive Dissonance

You will know this feeling if you have ever noticed something "off" about a situation but you can't quite put your finger on it. As I've described in previous books, a spy's job is to notice baselines and norms in all situations so they know when something is amiss. When something isn't right it sets off a level of dissonance in the mind and subsequently triggers a response to act to make it right. People with OCD also know this feeling well as they might insist on having their desk arrangement a certain way for example, a pen pot or hole punch even a few inches out of place will cause a cognitive dissonance in their mind until the object is moved back to its original place. In fact cognitive dissonance is the process by which we naturally experience any real changes or differences in the world around us.

However the level of this dissonance also increases with the perceived importance of the situation, how far away the current position is compared to the original and lastly our perceived inability to rationalize the discrepancy away. For this reason, a cognitive dissonance conflict in our mind can be a very effective motivator for behavioral change. It is the most effective and productive way to release the tension and rectify the dissonance that exists. The other way would be to not change the behavior but instead justify it by changing the conflicting cognition or adding new ones to alleviate the old problem. In general terms this just means rationalizing the conflict away in your mind so it no longer affects you in the way it previously did.

Dissonance is also much more apparent when it comes to issues on self-image, nobody wants to feel stupid, immoral etc so a projection of one of these feelings can be a powerful trigger for behavior change. As a result, cogitative dissonance can play a very large and central role in the persuasion process or any attempt to change behaviors, values and beliefs. This dissonance tension can be applied in both acute bursts or over a longer sustained period of time. It works much like the reverse psychology principle I described above, and it is your job to find the cognitive norms in people's minds and disrupt them to a point where they want to make the behavioral change to fix it.

Counter-Attitudinal Advocacy

It is common place for people to state a view on something or support an opinion that they do not necessarily believe to be true themselves. This isn't as deceptive as it may sound as the things people do this with are often very small and well intended, like a white lie told to protect someone's feelings or where their own views maybe offensive in a situation. When this happens, we attempt to reduce the dissonance caused by justifying our actions as noble.

Now whether you believe this to be acceptable or that total and open honesty is the best course of action is irrelevant as you can use this natural human tendency to your advantage when persuading others. I have seen this happen within certain cults around the world and within gangs when changing people's beliefs to justify their behavior change in a more sinister way.

This persuasion principle like many others, actually ties in very closely with another which is "Incremental Escalating Requests." The idea is to offer the person very small rewards so that they do not attribute their behavior to any real change. But over time this effect escalates to a point where they are doing something radically different from where they started.

Try to do this in practice yourself, get people to go along with you on small points but on things that are directed towards the eventual persuasion goal. Make sure the points are small enough so that the internal justification for agreeing with you on them isn't significant enough for them to question or resist. After sometime, their beliefs should start to change to yours.

Perceived Self-Interest

As much as humans like to believe that they are generous and caring creatures, there is no getting away from the fact that we can ultimately be very self-serving as a species. Many experiments concerning game theory such as the "prisoner's dilemma" prove this time and again. Psychologists even argue that altruism is a self-serving act as by performing a task purely for another person's benefit (with seemingly no pay for ourselves) is actually only an attempt to garner the feel good factor we get from the empathy we receive as a result.

The idea on this one is simple, it is all about perception. If you can convince somebody to believe (whether it's true or not) that what they are doing is in their own best interest, then they are much more likely to go along with it. This is especially apparent when it comes to persuading or impressing people of higher stature than you, like your boss or employer. Say something like "I see my job as making you more successful" or "If I can make your life easier then I have done my job". This will endear a new or prospective employee to a boss greatly, as although you will gain some credit along the way, ultimately you do not want to steal the limelight too heavily from there person who pays your wages.

But as always, remember to do this in a genuine and tactful manner. You do not want to come across as being purely brown nosing as that will likely showcase your own WIIFM ("What's in it for me") thinking.

Disrupt-Then-Reframe (DTR)

This strategy is very similar to the "Offer Biasing" and "Russian Front" negotiation tactics I described within my book on the same subject. It's all about assessing norms once more and disrupting the way in which people think along those lines.

The idea is to put out a statement that is very far away from what the person's beliefs and ideals are to begin with. This is like offering them something they are very unlikely to want or accept. Then you follow this up with a much more rational request that the person will likely go along with as they are still making the comparison to the first one in their mind. This second suggestion will obviously be the one you are looking to persuade them towards.

It's a little like reverse tagging however it's performed in a slightly longer statement which you are also rephrasing and disrupting what you are saying. It can even be something nonsensical in nature as the aim is to just disrupt what is being said and being thought first and foremost.

Two researchers at the university of Arkansas Barbara Price and Eric Knowles put this theory to the test when they set up an experiment in which they would offer customers note cards by door to door sellers from some invented nonprofit organization for disabled children. The sellers would initially introduce themselves and their sales pitch before asking if the person would like to know the price of the cards. In some instances this disruption phrase was applied, in this case offering the cards "for 300 pennies" before stating, "that's just 3 dollars, it's a bargain!" The studies found that the DTR sales pitches were anywhere from 1.5-2 times more likely to convert when compared to the normal sales pitch.

This approach is based primarily on the studies of hypnotist Milton Erikson and his methods of deliberately disrupting peoples waking thought patterns and behaviors that would destabilize their habitual thinking and change it while the person was still somewhat unsure of what to think next. It's a kind of confusion tactic that allows you just enough time to reframe what the other person is thinking in a "hurt and rescue" type fashion.

This leads me onto the final persuasion tactic…

Hurt and Rescue principle

Again much like the "Russian Front" style negotiation tactic, the "Hurt and Rescue" principle is based off of evoking a level of fear or discomfort in the person initially. Then when they are assessing their options for other solutions, you offer them the one you are trying to persuade them towards. It's a way of manufacturing a level of discomfort before offering some form of relief from it.

Again like everything I'm suggesting in this book, be careful not to come across as intimidating or aggressive which can set off a 'fight or flight' response in the person that will be massively counterproductive here. This should in fact just be a subtle nudge in the right direction when done correctly.

You can say something like "I've noticed that you performance has dropped off recently to the point where we might have to cut your funding. Don't worry; I've convinced my seniors not to do that so long as you start meeting the metrics again."

This is done all of the time in criminal and law enforcement negotiations and interrogations. The accused suspect will regularly be painted the picture of long jail time and harsh treatment before being offered the plea deal in exchange for more favorable terms.

CHAPTER 4

SPY TACTICS FOR HIGH-PRESSURE/STAKES SITUATIONS

As a spy, I had to face some high-pressure situations where communication above all else was my biggest weapon. Some of these situations arose during my interviews and training and but many while out on the job. However it was always critical to keep a calm composure and make the most of the situation even when things looked dire.

One of the worst things you can do in a high pressure situation is to show the other party that you are uncomfortable. In my line of work, losing your composure is one of the quickest ways to blow your cover. In casual or business interactions, losing your composure can show everything from nervousness, fear, and a general lack of confidence.

The key to keeping your composure is in suppressing the 'fight or flight' response I have mentioned previously. Anxiety can also cause this. From the second adrenaline starts pumping through your system, your ability to perceive the situation shrinks. You will lose focus and be unable to think clearly. It can also cause a rapid heartbeat, sweating, and an array of other unwanted symptoms. You should avoid this at all costs.

The following is a guide on how you can control a situation such as this and the qualities you need to possess in order to tackle these instances effectively.

Communication

Communication is obviously the central theme to persuasion in general and in turn this book, but it is especially important when it comes to controlling a high-pressure situation. You have to start to think of things in a very elementary way. You will have to be in a position to explain something to someone in such a way that they will be able to explain it back to you without difficulty. That is how strong and clear your communication skills should be here. You must make use of clear language that uses only simple words and phrases for clarity that are not ambiguous or confusing in anyway. Think of everybody in the room as having only a beginner's grasp on the language you are speaking. This will force you to break it down to the clearest and most concise steps. Often times this would be me, speaking Russian in a room of Mafia members or Portuguese with government officials in Lisbon. Do not use overly complicated phrases which could be misinterpreted or misunderstood.

I often tell the story about my dealings with a section of the Russian mafia who were based out of Hungary at the time, in the capital Budapest to be precise. The story is actually more concerned with the exit strategy I had to employ to escape without getting killed. To quickly re-cap, I was held up in a tight spot trying to arrange a price for some unregistered guns I was trying to sell to this outfit. Things went bad pretty quickly and I ended up using a pre-planned escape route where an extraction team was waiting to fetch me out.

What I don't usually tell people is how the situation deteriorated to that point as in reality it is quite embarrassing for me to admit in truth. Russians can be difficult to deal with at the best of times and especially when they are suspicious or in a highly charged and vodka induced emotional state (which this crew definitely was at the time). It basically came down to communication or a lack of sufficient clarity on my part. My Russian was reasonably strong at this point, not as fluent as my Portuguese after spending considerable time in Brazil in the late 1990's before being the Lisbon station chief in the early 2000's.

But it was good enough to get by. However I had picked up somewhat of an unwanted habit after dating a local girl whilst based in St. Petersburg just a few years prior. Russians have a tendency to add diminutive suffixes to words that we can't really do in English. They often put these before nouns to make them softer sounding, for example "chik" will turn any masculine noun into something way less serious. There are lots of these suffixes and my girlfriend would use them all of the time. Now this is where it went bad for me, as I decided it would be a good idea to start using this type of language with the mafia guys in an attempt to soften the situation. I actually think I started to use the feminine "chka" by mistake. Needless to say it didn't work and these

45

chaps took it as more of an insult to their masculinity more than anything. So that game and experiment was over for me that day but not without learning a serious lesson, always stick to the most basic, clear and least misinterpret able words possible in high stakes situations..."

Preparation

I'm big on preparation as you have probably already realized and the high stakes persuasion game is no different. One of the best ways to tackle a high-pressure situation is to be 100% be prepared for it. By remaining prepared for a situation, you will know what to say and do and what phrases to fall back on. Also you will be acutely aware of what your intensions and purpose were in the first place to remain focused and on track.

I have stated this before, but as a spy, most of the work that I did was based on psychological warfare. For interrogation, information extraction, or other reasons, learning about the individual and subsequently using psychological techniques to get what was needed was paramount. You had to research your mark and learn all you could, finding out how they will respond to various personality traits & behavioral patterns. Then adapt your own behavior accordingly to optimally get the most out of them.

So in order to effectively persuade someone especially in high stakes settings, you will have to anticipate the situation and know exactly how someone is likely to react ahead of time. Combing this type of preparation with quick thinking and advanced persuasion skills is the recipe for winning here.

Adaptable Behavior

Remember that your behavior matters most in a situation like this. You will find that individual situations, as in life, especially these high stakes settings are never completely cut and dry. Regardless of your preparation, things will never go entirely how you anticipated, and that's OK. Remember that our body language counts for a lot and drives across the message to the other person for whatever emotions you are portraying. You need not necessarily to be in a powerful position in order to control a high-pressure situation as it is flexibility that matters more. You have to be able to adapt and do more behavior-wise in order to persuade someone.

Your personality should also be flexible enough to react and be able to call on the intuitive and relational persuasion skills you have built up. If you notice, children can be very persuasive as they have an array of habits to fall back on while trying to convince someone of something. Say a child wants a piece of candy; he will pout, cry, throw a tantrum, plead and even plant a kiss in order to get it. The parent, however, will have just one response to give which is saying "no" to the child. Similarly, you will only be able to control a situation if you showcase an array of behaviors that will garner the right response from your opponent and ultimately have command over the situation through your behavioral flexibility. Try to cultivate this into your thinking and practice adaptability wherever you can. Try to incorporate this into your day-to-day, when the stakes aren't high.

Emotions

Remember to leash your emotions as best you can during high-pressure situations. I talk a lot about how emotions can't be avoided during my discussion of negotiation principles, but that is more about inducing empathy in the everyday interactions we have. When it comes to highly charged high pressure situations it's a different story.

When these situations come about, most people will turn into becoming vulnerable. They will not be able to control their emotions and cause the situation to get out of hand. In such a case, it will be important to stay calm and not give away a negative reaction. This is, of course, easier said than done and will be important to remain patient. You will have to read a situation correctly and ensure that you know how to control your emotions. Remain as detached from it as possible so that your emotions lie well within your control.

Strong Belief

If you are sure about yourself and remain confident then you are much more likely to control a situation and persuade your opponent more effectively. Confidence and certainty are two important qualities to possess when it comes to persuading someone (which I'll describe in greater detail within the following chapters).

You have to be able to exude confidence so that the other person knows you are certain, people can relate to assertiveness and assurance in someone's mannerisms very easily and it will put everybody at ease especially in high stakes settings. With time and practice, you will be able to identify when these intense situations are likely to come about. You will be in a more comfortable position to persuade people when they do.

PART 2:

CONVERSATIONAL STRATEGIES & PERSONALITY TRAITS TO WIN OVER EVEN THE TOUGHEST ADVERSARY

CHAPTER 5

CULTIVATING A LIKABLE & CHARISMATIC PERSONALITY

Nothing beats charm and confidence when it comes to impressing or persuading someone. If you are trying to win a person over or persuade them of something then you will have to work on your personality first and foremost. Even the toughest adversary can be won over with a little charm if you know how to use it. In order to help you out with this, I have written this segment that will cover topics such as building character, charisma, personality, charm etc. As a spy, I often had to make use of these qualities in order to win over a situation, it comes with the territory. So I have compiled the following chapters based on my experiences so you may do the same.

A charismatic personality is liked by one and all. It will help a person to attain almost everything they are trying to achieve in life. Interaction and people skills absolutely cannot be avoided in the real world. To some people this will come more naturally especially if they were brought up in an environment where witty and comedic conversation was common place either within their family and/or friends circle. To others it might take a little more practice to develop the charismatic talking tools and personality traits conducive for successful persuasion. But you might as well start somewhere, so here is look at the different elements that contribute towards developing a charismatic and likable personality that is so important to acquire.

Gestures

Be it the nod of the head or the shaking of hands, your gestures speak volumes about your personality. Everybody likes a person who uses their body language to their full advantage. You are looking for firm, intentional movements here. If you are trying to impress someone, then it will also be important to be as open with your body as possible. A closed body will not drive across the right message. Shake your hands, raise them, signal with them as you speak, nod your head to affirm you're in agreement to a question; use your facial expressions for the same effect etc. Practice these in front of a mirror to know how they look. It will give you a boost of confidence to carry out these gestures in front of others. But ensure that you don't overdo it. You might come across as a very restless person if you end up showing too much energy which is counter to what you are trying to achieve here.

Confidence

The importance of cultivating high level confidence in relation to achieving anything in life cannot be overstated; it's the reason I wrote my first book on exactly that topic. This is why I won't go into any major detail here. Needless to say, you can only develop high level confidence when you have full trust in yourself. This comes down to practice and preparation like anything else, knowing your strategies to cultivate an over arching self-confidence whilst also knowing the tricks to overcome situational social anxiety and self-doubt when they may arise. Having confidence in yourself within any interaction and especially important persuasion and negotiation situations goes without saying.

Some of these strategies include overcoming limiting beliefs, stacking your skills, doing your homework, having an exit strategy, dressing the part, exercising regularly and being adaptable. Once you have these skill sets down you will operate optimally in literally every situation you find yourself in, and especially high stakes persuasion.

Vocal Expression

A lot can be expressed via the human voice, we seem to be the only species that has developed the complex structures in the larynx, like the vocal chords etc to successfully produce language. It is possible for you to modulate your voice and control everything from volume, pitch to intonation, so you should do it. Vocally expressing your emotion can win someone over, whether it is joy or sadness or excitement that you want to express, your voice can serve as a great tool. This is especially useful during phone conversations where you will not be able to showcase your gestures. You will have only your voice to convince or persuade the other person and this will require some level of modulation through the course of the conversation. As I mentioned above, the three most important aspects to modulate are the tone, pitch and volume. So make sure you practice with various vocal expressions during everyday conversations to see what reactions you get in preparing for when it matters most.

Center of Attention

I know this will come with improvements on the confidence side but in the mean time try not to run away from the spotlight and take it when it comes. I know this will seem to run counter to the other advice I give i.e. staying out of any provocative situations but you do need some training for when they may arise. The more naturally introverted amongst us tend to try and escape these situations, as they are unsure of themselves.

But being the center of attention can work in your favor, as you will be able to showcase an array of likeable personality traits to a group of people especially if you can hold the room. In fact, the spotlight tends to bring out the best in people and makes them stronger for it, it's an extremely character building process. When mastered, it also shows that you can handle the pressure of other human attention and judgment. You too can use it to express yourself better and be in a position to persuade others around you more effectively when it's required.

Dress the Part

Pay very close attention to what you wear. Your general attire will tell people who you actually are. If you wish to come across as someone who should be taken seriously then you have to dress accordingly. How confident in persuading someone would you feel if you spent a business meeting adjusting your shirt, because it didn't fit you well? How clearly could you think with shoes pinching your toes? Like acting the part, dressing the part will help you feel confident and sure of yourself as you go about your business. As you dress, think about how other people would dress. If you have a meeting with a specific company or are interviewing, choose a position-appropriate outfit.

You should also consider how you want people to perceive you. Whether you admit it or not, your mind subconsciously judges people on the way that they are dressed. The way you act upon this initial perception is up to you, but it's very difficult to discount this first impression. If you dress in well-fitting clothes that are clean, you will come across as someone who has their life together and exude natural gravitas.

Something to remember as you choose your clothes though is to stay comfortable. You will not be able to give the persuasion process the attention it needs if you cannot focus because your clothes aren't comfortable. Choose clothes, shoes, and accessories that fit well and that are appropriate for how you want people to perceive you. Pick out your clothes at least a couple of days prior, in case you find that something doesn't fit well or needs to be cleaned before your occasion.

Whilst your outward facing image/appearance to the world isn't what will ultimately make the difference is persuading people in your life, that comes down to talking tools mostly. It does however have a knock-on effect to your confidence and charisma in general that certainly won't hurt the process.

The Storyteller

Apart from your physical appearance and gestures, it is also how you speak to others and what you tell them that will influence them greatly. Become a good storyteller and tell people interesting and intriguing anecdotes. Use humor as much as you can in order to make it interesting for others. Remain up to date with news and current affairs so that you are able to use these in your stories.

"The object of oratory alone is not truth, but persuasion"

(Thomas B. Macaulay)

The ability to tell a good story can come in handy in a number of situations. You can use it to allude to a presentation, break the ice for a business meeting or date, or answer a question in an interview. I've had many situations in both my professional and civilian life where this has come in handy. Usually, it was used as a stalling tactic if my cover was about to be compromised. If things were going bad, a few canned anecdotes would often give you enough room to maneuver out of situation or even an extraction team time to step in if things really got hairy.

The ability to be a good story teller is also a very interesting and attractive personality trait in and of itself. It can smooth the tension in many situations especially if you are thrown into a center of attention situation I described above. Do your best to practice telling a few stories that you can fall back on in different situations that you may find yourself in. It will certainly help with your persuasive powers when it matters most.

Avoid Distractions (Exist in the Moment)

Having too many distractions and giving into them can eat away at your charisma. Right from checking your phone to watching television there can be many distractions around us. You have to be able to keep these distractions at bay and focus on your job at hand, i.e. being a good communicator.

You cannot give an amazing presentation nor have a great date if you are constantly wondering how it is going to end or wondering what the other party is thinking. When you are involved in something like a persuasive conversation, it is important that you give it your entire focus. Do your best to exist in the moment paying close attention to the body language of other people, as well as your own.

While you should exist in the moment, it's also a good idea to think just one or two steps ahead. Being prepared for questions you may be asked or making small talk will prepare you for this. Thinking ahead a few seconds into the future if you are anticipating questions or another response is a wise tactic if it doesn't take you out of the present moment. However, do not think so far ahead that you are worrying about what is going to happen instead of focusing on the task at hand.

As a spy, you have to learn to both exist in the moment and think a few steps ahead. The importance of being able to pick up on crucial cues and being able to react to the situation goes without saying. This has a lot to do with reading the people around you, paying close attention to their body language and how they are reacting to what you have to say, which is critical within a persuasive environment. Information you cannot fully absorb if you are not intensely present.

CHAPTER 6

IMPORTANCE OF SMALL TALK

The importance of small talk is often understated. People don't realize how important it is to talk to others on a daily basis and not just on the big things, which is why I have dedicated an entire chapter to it. This includes all people that we come across on a day-to-day basis colleagues, acquaintances and total strangers alike.

Small talk is an incredibly useful habit. Basically, you should be talking to everyone! That may sound like a cheesy sound bite from a telecom commercial but it's true. If you are going on a date, meeting, or other important occasion, start by talking to the 'peripheral' people in and around the building. This is especially useful if you are naturally more introverted. Some of the people you may talk to include door staff, secretaries, waiters, and anyone else you encounter leading up to the event.

The benefits to doing this are twofold. The first is that it loosens you up and gets you ready to converse. This is especially beneficial if you have approach or social anxiety, because it gets you in the rhythm of interacting with people. The second benefit of small talk is that you might pick up on some important nugget of information that you wouldn't have otherwise gotten. This can be very beneficial when it comes to persuasion and negotiation situations. It might be something small that can help you interact with the person or organization you are about to meet with. If a secretary tells you that the guy you are waiting for is late due to dropping his boy off at soccer practice, slip into your conversion with him how you love watching your own kids play soccer! You don't even have to have any...

This is something that is incredibly useful when you are a spy, particularly when it comes to picking up interesting tidbits of information. When you are collecting intelligence on a person or organization, talking to people who may know of them was mandatory. I have alluded to this story before, but I remember one time that I was trying to speak with a CEO of a large company I was gathering intelligence on. He was less than willing to talk to me. When I had asked to speak to him, his secretary said he had already left. I tried my luck with various people around the building, even the attendant of the parking lot. He was quite puzzled when he pointed out the CEO's parking spot, which was filled with his car. I waited him out and eventually got to do my questioning.

So in this chapter, we will take a look at understanding the true meaning and importance of small talk.

What is small talk?

Small talk essentially refers to having a casual conversation on topics that are not of any real significance to the people involved. It is carried out to open conversations, gauge peoples current mood and a means to understand others and get their perspective on a particular topic.

People tend to take a liking to those that open up and speak out. One good way of doing this is by indulging in small talk. Small talk refers to striking up a conversation with strangers in order to establish a connection. It's very much related to the previous chapter regarding creating a likeable and charismatic personality, it also very much helps build empathy and rapport which are essential for productive and harmonious interactions of all kinds. Also the more contacts you establish, the bigger your circle will be and the more people you can call upon when needed. So try to speak to as many different people as possible in order to expand your influence. My preference was to always develop a considerable network of contacts of all descriptions where ever I was based in the world and I attribute a large part of my success to pulling from that knowledge base when I needed it.

Start Small

Start by talking to the people that surround you. In a day, we come across several acquaintances and usually settle for just hi or hello or even a nod of the head. You must make it a point to take it to the next level and start a conversation. Pick a topic and ask them their opinion on it. Try to have at least a 5-minute conversation with them and get their opinion on something.

Be Curious

Try to remain as curious as possible when talking to different people. Do not stick to the same old set of people but rather anybody that you may come across. This very importantly includes strangers. Look out for interesting people around you and strike up a conversation where you can. The more you do it, the more confidence you will gain from it. Approach them in a way that makes them comfortable. It can be as simple as asking for directions and then having a small conversation.

Body Language

Ensure you maintain positive body language. This means that you respect their personal space but still appear confident. Use your hands to gesture and facial expressions to entice them. Try to bring in as much variety into your conversations as possible. Read their body language to judge if they are being open to you and interested in carrying forward the conversation.

Be Interesting

Without needing to be a comedian you still have to make the interaction as interesting as possible so that the other person feels motivated to continue with it. Pick up on diverse topics that are bound to solicit a reaction. News and current affairs make for great topics to discuss. I always look out for sports clothing where a person is wearing their favorite teams hat or jersey before commenting on how they played that week. Everybody likes to moan about their teams form or the state of the weather. Of course you need to know a little about the subject to do this but the same concept applies to anything that the person is obviously interested in and passionate about, so use it when you see it.

Pretensions

It is important to be yourself and drop any pretensions. If you try to put on an act then it will make the other person uncomfortable and question your credibility. You must refrain from coming across as aloof as it will likely annoy the other person also. They too will start becoming pretentious and the conversation will not be a fruitful one.

The Importance of Small Talk

Intel Gathering

As I mentioned in the opening remarks to this chapter, indulging in small talk can greatly help with gathering information. Right from knowledge of what the other person has been doing to getting the latest news on a persuasion adversary, vital information can be obtained. People always tend to let things slip during these otherwise meaningless chit chat sessions and especially if they like you. Again this is why it's important to be charismatic and build that rapport with everyone you speak with. You never know how this information can help you.

It is, therefore, a great idea to indulge in small talk and do it with everyone. If you wish to get them to tell you something of interest then you must be willing to divulge something yourself. It doesn't have to be anything especially important, just something about your habits or life so that they open up and start to reciprocate. Then you can slowly massage the conversation onto more critical topics employing the "Counter-Attitudinal Advocacy" & "Incremental Escalating Requests" strategies I have already described to really get what you need.

Confidence Building

As I have already mentioned, small talk is great for building general confidence. You will come into contact with many types of people who will all add to your confidence if you speak with them when you cross paths, especially if you are the one to approach them in order to strike up the conversation. This will certainly be of benefit to introverts who are ordinarily unable to speak freely with others. Small talk will provide a great platform to conquer social anxiety and be open to other people in general.

Likeability Factor

By talking to everyone, you will be able to increase your likeability factor greatly. People will be drawn to you and approach you confidently to strike up a conversation. It will add to your personality traits and increase your appeal. It's like a positive feedback loop, increased confidence will increase your likeability which in turn will increase the amount of conversations and interactions you will have.

This will all feed into your own feel good factor and snow ball your efforts even further. Human beings tend to feel lighter when they have conversations as we are innately social creatures who thrive off of interaction. Studies show a high level of dopamine release within the brain after productive and enjoyable conversations. So regardless of whom you are talking to, speaking out about something is bound to make you feel better about yourself. So in order to feel good and find this release, just strike up small talk with everyone and anyone you can find.

CHAPTER 7

POWER OF IMPECCABLE GREETINGS AND GOOD LANGUAGE

"He who wants to persuade should put his trust not in the right argument, but in the right word. The power of sound has always been greater than the power of sense"

(Joseph Conrad)

There are a few tricks you can employ as a good communicator which will always ensure interactions go better than expected, and these include performing really positive and impactful greetings (as well as goodbyes) and using impeccable language. Greetings and goodbyes are especially important as they book end or sandwich the conversation in a way that can heighten a person's perception of you if you do them well. If you really nail the start and finish of the interaction, that is what the person will remember most, even if the meat of what you were saying wasn't necessarily very compelling.

The first thing to note is to make sure you always address people by their name; it's the most satisfying sound anybody can hear. I never understood people who would perennially claim that "Oh, I'm not good with names" or "I can remember faces really well though". I'm afraid that this won't cut it if you are trying to make a lasting impression. It's literally just a case of a little hard work in memory improvement, so don't be lazy. I had many memory tricks and systems for recalling pieces of information in the field and one specifically to remember names. I would play a kind of rhyming association game in my head with some piece of information about the person or how we had met "Coffee Shop Kerry" or "Boston Bradley". It sounds trivial but remembering by association will really imprint the information deep in those synapses instead of surface level recollection that almost always gets forgotten.

When you first meet the person try to avoid any peripheral distractions as this is your only time to really commit this to memory. Ask them to state and even repeat their name to fully get it. It's actually easier when it comes to more obscure or ambiguous names as you can ask them to spell it out. "S-T-E-P-H-I-E or do you spell it with a Y?" It's a bit more difficult to do this with a Rob or Dave of course. But doing this will ensure that not only will you commit it to memory more efficiently, but will also show you are genuinely interested in them. Then it's never a bad idea to repeat the name where you can throughout the initial conversation to further imbed it into your memory as well as building more rapport.

First Impressions

Making a good first impression in general is extremely important. As you know, perception is everything and people are going to judge you based on your opening impression. Be it within the friend circle, at your workplace or while meeting a stranger, it is important to get this right. How you speak and carry yourself is how you will be perceived and your aim should be to leave a lasting impression on the listener.

From the moment someone first sees you, their mind will start to assess you and make judgments. This is why it is also important to dress well, smell good, and be well-groomed whenever you have an important presentation, date, or meeting. In addition to all of these things, you want to take the steps to build a great rapport and give off an air of confidence, letting everyone know that you are sure of yourself. As you greet everyone, address him or her by name if you know them. If not, employ the memory recollecting tactic I explained above. You should also practice good, strong handshakes and making eye contact with people. These are all habits that confident people use and it will show that you are a strong person who is sure of themselves. It will put everybody at ease.

Greetings

Greeting people the right way is extremely important. You must say the right things in order to give them a positive impression of you. Greetings are powerful expressions that you can use to influence others. Here is a look at how to do it correctly.

- As you see the person approaching, stand straight. Ensure you are not being fidgety. Do not place your hands in pocket and keep them free.

- If you are sitting down then stand up and acknowledge them.

- Greet them with a pleasant smile.

- Shake their hand firmly whilst making strong eye contact.

- Say "hi" or "hello" in a friendly manner. It is best to stick with "hello" if it is a formal meeting. Its how the British do it and they invented the language!

- Tell them it's nice to make their acquaintance and state your name clearly and ask for theirs. Spell it out if it's conducive to do so.

- Don't hesitate to ask them something again if it wasn't clear the first time. Tell them they were too fast or slow and you couldn't understand what they said.

- Finally, end the greeting on a positive note. You must try to part by leaving a smile on the person's face. If you do these steps effectively, they won't forget it.

Elements of good language

It goes without saying that language breaks barriers and brings people closer together as a society in general. By communicating in language that is clear and well understood, we have the chance to bridge gaps and build the relationships required for effective persuasion. But in order to do so, we must first understand the basics of good language and how something as simple as a greeting we looked at above, can help you with being a top class communicator.

Here is look at some elements of good language.

Communication

Having a good command over language will help you with every aspect of communication, period. In my career I came across a wide variety of people and the only way to keep them engaged was by making use of great language skills. These skills were acquired over the years and not developed overnight. I realized pretty early on that it is only through good and clear language that I would be able to communicate with others to get what I needed. You too must develop a clear communication style, one that can be easily understood by others. Simple and agreeable is usually the best place to start.

Vocabulary

Vocabulary of course just refers to the knowledge and usage of words. The broader your lexicon, the better your overall communication will be. I have told the following story many times but it is equally apt here. Imagine you want to become a lawyer and that you were casually talking to an experienced group of them as they started to tell industry specific jokes and filled them with confusing vocabulary only used in law cases. It's likely that you wouldn't understand what they were saying, and your chance of being taken seriously would be slim.

Learning the common vocabulary is always something I did before approaching anybody with any level of importance or any gatekeeper to what I needed to achieve. People in every field of work/life will use certain terminology which if you do not know, will highlight you as an amateur and pretty quickly at that. This is bad news if you are trying to get a leg up in that interview or meeting. Try to attain at least a base level of competence by reading around your given industry as much as possible. Read the articles and blogs your persuasion opponents would read as they will talk in the vocabulary most common to them in those publications.

During my first few months in the CIA, I was involved in a number of operations on US soil as a warm up for more difficult foreign ops. This included being shipped to the outer parts of the Washington D.C. area, in a pretty rough neighborhood. The idea was that I would go undercover in a local street gang dealing in high end stolen cars. Think of the movie "Gone in 60 Seconds" but way less glamorous.

At first glance, I definitely don't look like I belong in a professional car stealing outfit. I am of fairly average height. I'm a muscular build, but not too heavily set. I have a five o'clock shadow most of the day, plain brown hair. Oh, and I wear glasses, at least I did when I was working the desk job. I don't have any special kind of look; I'm just your average looking guy. My objective was to infiltrate the gang, finding out what I could about their operation. I have to admit that when I put on the clothes I was supposed to wear, I felt ridiculous. They had suited me in a tracksuit and a baggy white t-shirt. I wore contacts for this one, since glasses would be hard to keep on if I ended up in any high speed chases. This proved to be a good idea.

In the end getting a foot in the door with these guys wasn't that difficult as I was easily able to hotwire a car and steal it as my induction. It was more the lingo they spoke and vocabulary they used that would give me away.

The guys in charge of the operation made sure I looked the part, but I also had to act the part. A lot of this was learning the lingo. Gang members at this level were incredibly cautious of new people and the slightest slip in my personality could mean blowing my cover. I spent weeks researching top end car specs, even pulling a few guys in off the nearby streets that owed me favors, to make sure I really spoke their language.

Now this is more of a case of speak the 'right' language, having a broad vocabulary and good speaking style will serve you well in all situations. However you need to be able to identify what situations require more technical talk and when you need to be more straight to the point, and of course fluid enough to adapt to different situations accordingly. It's not only the words and phrases you use either, it's your expressions whilst you do it. I touched on this within the previous chapter, but your gestures and body language also need to be congruent with what you are saying.

Mastering the art of good language and speaking skills will help you in literally every avenue of life. From career, school, social life to everything in between. Politicians or anybody who holds a position of influence for that matter aren't always the smartest amongst us, they are just the best speakers. You don't have to orate like Winston Churchill or Franklin D. Roosevelt to win people over, but improving your language and speaking skills even moderately will help you immeasurably.

CHAPTER 8

IMPORTANCE OF BEING A GREAT LISTENER

So whilst having already reviewed the importance of good language and speech, it's time to look at the other side of the communication coin which is equally critical to productive communication. Listening to someone is just as important as speaking to them, if not more so. So much goes misunderstood or misinterpreted as a result of things not being heard right in interactions of all nature. I'll spare you the clichéd statements of having two ears and one mouth etc but they certainly do ring true.

My career with the CIA was built on many different facets but in reality there were only really a few key skill sets, one of them was becoming a professional listener. I had to pay keen attention to people and what they had to say all of the time. It was important to pick up on things that were being spoken about themselves and others and any other important information that they would inadvertently give away. People make it more complicated than it has to be at times, I promise you, if you truly listen to what somebody is saying you will know what they are thinking. Very few people can truly mask what's in their thoughts with what they are saying, it's harder than you think and I was trained to spot this happening. The vast majority of people in everyday civilian life will be as forthcoming as can be, so pay attention and listen to what they are saying when they speak.

Here are just some of the benefits of developing this trait for yourself.

- By paying attention to what others are saying, you will be able to contribute to the conversation in a much more efficient way. You can build on themes faster without constant reiteration of points.

- Similar to the above, paying keen attention helps with understanding the situation and the problem and coming up with a solution much quicker.

- You will be acquainted with different perspectives. Things that you may not have previously considered.

- By truly listening to others you have the chance to pick up on important peripheral information that may not have originally been apparent.

- Listening carefully allows you to avoid misunderstandings and potential conflicts. You will have a clear understanding of what the other person is saying and not be confused.

- By listening carefully you will be able to better recollect the information especially if it was only spoken word.

- Listening properly helps greatly in enhancing relationships. It's a great rapport builder as we've already seen.

These are just some of the countless uses of listening carefully. They are also some elements to take into consideration to make sure you are doing it right.

Distractions

The first and most important step is to do away with any distractions. If there are distractions around you then they are bound to command your attention. You must try to get rid of them so that you can pay full attention to the person in front of you. If someone approaches you when you are carrying out an important task, then kindly ask them to wait until you are done so that you can pay full attention to them. If you are in the middle of a big crowd and cannot listen to someone properly then step aside with them in order to listen carefully. As a rule, it is important not to look over them as that can make them uncomfortable.

Body language

Pay attention to their body language. As you know, communication is not about speaking alone and involves many other factors such as physical gestures, facial expressions etc. You must pay attention to all these factors in order to understand whether a person is comfortable speaking with you or uncomfortable. As I say, it's very difficult for somebody to truly mask what they are thinking or how they are feeling. You will be able to tell whether they are excited, restless or feeling dull and tired. For example, if the person has crossed their arms it is indicative of a defensive approach to the conversation. They might be hiding some information or refrain from divulging it.

Tone, Pitch, Volume

It will be important to pay attention to their tone and pitch as well as how loudly somebody is speaking. This will be a clear indication of the person's true mood. If the pitch is high then it indicates excitement. If they are speaking in a low pitch then it indicates that the person is not necessarily motivated greatly by what they are saying. If it's also in a low volume range then it would also suggest a lack of authority with louder speaking conveying the opposite.

Of course you need to be familiar with the person and their natural speaking style to truly gauge these factors from their usual baseline norms. The tone can also reveal the emotion behind the person's conversation. Speaking in a lower or creaking tone will often signal inferiority. If they are maintaining a consistent tone and speaking more fluently, this is associated with a more confident disposition. If the tone fluctuates by a large degree then be wary as it could mean that the person is not confident or potentially even lying to you.

Don't Interrupt

It goes without saying that if you really want to hear what the other person is saying then you will need to interrupt them as little as possible. Only do so when it's absolutely necessary as often times interrupting someone will ensure they lose the train of thought and can move you away from the topic at hand. You might say something that will confuse both of you. It will, therefore, be best to let the other person finish their monologue before adding in your inputs. Make a mental note of it and start addressing the points one by one as soon as the other person stops speaking. The same goes to the other person if they seem to be interrupting then ask them to kindly stop until you are done talking.

Silence

Learn to respect silence and the power that it brings forth. Many times, silence helps with understanding the other person better. Sometimes you can pick up more by what is not being said, by the gaps in between someone's speech. So don't be afraid of the pauses and silence. You will have the time to reflect on whatever has been said and come back with a reply. Although it might get a little uncomfortable when both of you remain silent, so entertain it long enough to know when the person has truly finished and when it's actually your time to chime in.

Mirror & Mimic

I talk about this in greater detail within "Negotiation. An Ex SPY's Guide" but it is always a good idea to mimic and mirror the other person to create a feeling of empathy. This is naturally done by the best persuaders and negotiators alike and you should further develop this trait within yourself as well. This should be done by matching the person's mannerisms and gestures as well as their speaking tone and style when it is your turn to talk. Don't just listen to what they are saying, pick up on the rhythm and energy and replicate their energy as they speak. But ensure you don't make it too obvious, like everything I suggest in this book, it should be done in a natural and subtle way.

CHAPTER 9

DEALING WITH INSULTS/ ARGUMENTS LIKE A PROFESSIONAL

Finally I wanted to include a chapter on the darker side of communication, the arguments/insults and how to deal with them. Now if you have taken note of everything else I have written on within this book and others then you should rarely if ever come across such situations as you will be a calm, confident, charismatic rapport builder. However unfortunately, sometimes these situations can be unavoidable. My job as strange as it may seem was to be a world class avoider of confrontation and conflict. Arguments or even violence was a big indication that an operation was failing to the point of last resort action. I was trained to see these things developing ahead of time and circumnavigate them before I got wrapped up into something that was difficult to escape from gracefully.

However as I mentioned, on rare occasions situations will turn up when an otherwise well intentioned conversation can turn confrontational. In this instance it's wise to know how to handle them ahead of time, a way to steer the ship to calmer waters. If a professional persuasion or negotiation starts to get heated then you have certainly failed in your objective. All bets are off as tempers rise along with the barriers to striking any agreements or deals.

But in everyday conversations I find I have a little more room to maneuver when it comes to dealing with argumentative behavior and insults directed toward me. So here is a look at some ways in which you can successfully deal with them when they come your way.

In general arguments and insults will largely fall into two main categories, rational/somewhat justified vs. irrational/personal attacks. I had to deal with both of these situations whilst in the field with the CIA and they both need to be dealt with in their own unique way. It should be fairly obvious which one you are dealing with when they come up so I will dive straight into the strategies for taking each on.

Rational & Justified

Now when I say that these are rational and justified all I really mean is that they are heated disputes against your position or proposal. These situations can arise from time to time and are not really a reflection of anything other than a significant disagreement.

This will be very close to the high pressure/stakes situations I described in an earlier chapter. These need to be handled with a clear head and logic. Firstly you need to assess what the other side is stating, do they have any validity to what they are saying? You need to assess your own positions and see if you have in fact done something to justify the accusations. Ask questions and use your listening skills to really understand what the other side's grievances really are.

You need to also look for win-wins in these situations, or make it seem like it in order so that you can buy time before properly appraising it. Remember always use clear and concise language when something is in contention. Respect what the other side is saying and reframe from interrupting.

Another useful linguistic tactic here is to use the "I agree" principle from negotiation. If somebody is stating a phrase like "I think you aren't giving us the best deal here". Simply reply "I agree, let's see how we can re-work this so everybody is happy". Now whether you really plan to re-negotiate or not, this is a wise thing to say. It's not about the facts and figures anymore but rather disarming the person of any psychological resistance to your next move/ statement and spark the urge within them to reciprocate in an agreeable way. It's a sound bite I use a lot when I get any objection to something. Try this in a heated argument and watch the response you get, nobody expects you to agree with them and it throws them off to a point of returning to rational discourse.

Irrational & Personal Attacks

You will likely know this category of attacks with much more familiarity; it's the type of irrational and hysterical attacks you see so often. I used to get into these altercations whilst under cover and there is a much more specific way to deal with them. Similar to the first category of arguments and insults you will come across, you need initially to stay very calm and clear headed.

The golden rule is to never get angry. Never let your emotions get to the point where you are acting out of anything other than a calculated and rational mindset. Just control your urge to raise your voice, as that will only worsen the scenario. Keep a tab on your body language and don't come across as intimidating. Inflated emotions will initiate the release of adrenaline and a cascade of other 'fight or flight' nervous system response hormones that will shrink perception and heavily reduce your ability to respond efficiently. Your biggest weapon in situations like this is clarity of thought, accepting what is going on and reacting by simply articulating your point. This brings me onto golden rule number two, disruption.

If the first weapon was clarity, the second is implementing a disruption or confusion tactic similar to the "I agree" principle above. In general you are looking to play a higher stakes game of "Disrupt and change" and other counterintuitive disarming techniques to empty any insult or attack of meaning. If you can show that the insult has no real logic or meaning then it has no power.

I had a colleague in the FBI who used to regularly get into bar fights in Boston, whenever somebody would say "Come outside and we'll settle this on the sidewalk" he would respond "But your car door is blue right, not yellow?" A statement like this is designed to take the other person out of the moment and back to something as mundane as the color of their car. It's like a momentary misdirection of thought, again based on Milton Erikson's disruption theories. Here you need to distract someone just long enough for the aggressor to snap out of the rage state and see sense. It's very difficult to resist doing this when somebody is mentioning something familiar to you. I have never seen an instance where this did not work for him.

The third tactic is humor. I'm not talking sarcastic back handed comments that are likely to inflate the situation even further, but rather making light of the situation to once again distract the person from the intensity of the situation. I don't tend to recommend this as freely as the misdirection approach as it's more difficult to get right, unless you have a very good grasp on comedic subtlety and handle on how far to push the situation. Otherwise as I mentioned, you can do more harm than good.

Lastly you can use the final tactic which is just to ignore what is going on. The first two tactics of thought misdirection and humor do require some quickness in thinking so will take some experience and practice, so just walking away can often be the best course of action. It's all about neutralizing things, escalating them doesn't make you strong; it just turns the situation into an untenable one where nothing productive can ever ensue. If it's prevalent to do so, just do not acknowledge the insult and move onto the next point. This will indicate that you are not concerned with going to that level and maintain a calm outlook on the interaction. This should also diffuse the situation enough prevent any further attacks.

Hopefully these will be enough to see you through any serious arguments. For me there was always one more level, when any of the above tactics didn't work out. That's a story for another book but let's just say the hand to hand combat training didn't always go to waste...

SUMMARY

Persuasion is one of the most important aspects of communication. It is necessary to convince others to listen to you in order to get them to work for you. To help you develop and hone your persuasion skills, this book should provide you with ample material designed to get you started on the right foot.

To start off, it's wise to understand the 6 basic principles or "weapons" of persuasion Cialdini describes, especially if you are in a commercial or marketing environment. They will help you understand the basic human psychological tendencies in behavior when it comes to influence and identify when you can employ them into your own situation. These principles have been tried and tested and accepted universally.

All human beings are motivated by one aspect of life or another. According to John Maslow, humans tend to follow a hierarchy when it comes to attaining life's goals. Understanding this hierarchy can help you lead a better life. Once you are aware of these basic physical and psychological motivators you will be able to assess people much more efficiently and have a better idea of what they may respond to.

There are different types of persuasion techniques that can be used to influence others and each one is applicable in a particular situation. All of them are based on theories that have either been tested through scientific study, my own personal experience and many times a combination of both. These include tactics such as "Reversal Tagging/Counter-Attitudinal Advocacy/Anchoring/Hurt and Rescue" just to name a few. Understanding them and using them in your daily life can help control situations to a certain extent and persuading others to listen to you. But consistency of application will be key and practice essential.

There will be many different situations that will arise in your day-to-day life where you will be required to use persuasion techniques. Being aware of these situations will prepare you to respond in a manner that will turn it around for you and work in your favor.

My life has been filled with high-pressure situations of all descriptions and in order to stay in control and remain in command of them, I had to make use of a certain skill set that supersedes normal and everyday discourse. Your communication needs to be crystal clear; you need to be well prepared having done your homework. You also need to be adaptable and while all of the time controlling your emotions. These skills should be developed as they are not inherently present in everyone. However with a little dedication and effort in the right direction, you will be able to develop and hone these skills so you can handle these high stakes situations when they come around.

It is no secret that everybody loves a charismatic personality, gravitas is difficult to defeat when it comes to the persuasion game. So you must try to develop your charms and use your personality to influence others where ever you can. There are certain basic personality enhancing elements to develop that will guide you through the process of persuasion such as improving vocal expressions and gestures, dressing the part and becoming a great story teller. Developing a strong personality can, in fact, make it extremely easy to influence others, as half the work will be taken care of for you.

Small talk is another important skill to develop in life. It's the glue in the fabric of conversations that allow you to move seamlessly from topic to topic. It also allows you the opportunity to talk with complete strangers or garner information you otherwise wouldn't have gotten. You must engage in small talk with everyone and anywhere you go. Keep it as interesting as possible and with time and practice, it will become progressively easier to carry out and your conversations will be exponentially more fruitful as a result.

When it comes to high level communication it is important to maintain the right type of language when you come in contact with people. What you say will say a lot about you, so make sure your vocabulary is broad and strong enough to stand the test. It's not always about good or impressive language either, it is equally important to taper what you are saying to the current audience. Use the lexicon and phrases they would use. Also never underestimate the impact of impeccable greeting and goodbyes. These are the things that people will remember the most so don't waste them with weak introductions or forgetting people's names.

It takes a lot of conscious skill and effort to be a good listener, to really indulge in what somebody is saying in a mindful manner. The majority of us do not take up this opportunity to learn what the other person is really telling us as we are either too easily distracted by things around us or simply just waiting for our term to talk. You need to really focus in to what the other person is saying and picking up on the details. This was one of my biggest weapons as a spy. Without realizing it, people tend to give away important information that can be of great use to you. You must remain ready to pick up on these hints and use it to your advantage.

If you manage to do all of the above correctly then you should be in a very good position when it comes to controlling interactions and persuasive conversations. However there will be rare occasions when things are maybe not so civil, when things get heated and you potentially have arguments and insults to deflect. The main trick here is in keeping your head, remaining calm and rationally being able to deal with what comes your way. Perception shrinks with every uptick in emotion so suppress that fight or flight urge to respond as such. Instead try to alter the persons thought patterns with a "Disrupt and change" strategy such as misdirection back to a mundane topic or the "I agree" principle.

CONCLUSION

I thank you for choosing this book and hope you had a good time reading it. The main aim was to educate you on all aspects of persuasion from the basic principles and psychological motivators, all the way to the more advanced and complex strategies and how you can use them to your advantage.

Many of the principles I have described will seem obvious and are things that you will do naturally, which is fine as it never hurts to recap on them. However many are not, they are counterintuitive mind tricks that require you to first understand and conceptualize before putting into practice.

Whilst you may have been tempted to read through these chapters at a high pace, it would be wise to go back and take some time on each of the individual principles for a second look, to study them one-by-one. This is the only way to effectively internalize the strategies and implement and master them individually before moving onto the next.

Only then can you start to stack these tactics one on top of another to genuinely become the highly competent persuader it's possible to be. I have done my bit by educating you on the art of persuasion. It is now entirely up to you to put this advice into practice in your day-to-day life. Everyone you come into contact with will be trying to exert some form of influence over you whether it's conscious or not, you can't escape it. You can simply decide if you are the one doing the persuading or the one being persuaded, the choice is now up to you...

All the best!

Negotiation

An Ex-SPY's Guide to Master the Psychological Tricks & Talking Tools to Become an Expert Negotiator in Any Situation

JAMES DAUGHERTY

TABLE OF CONTENTS

INTRODUCTION

Negotiation. Whenever people hear that word their mind naturally drifts towards the image of high level business deals being brokered, criminal hostage standoffs or politicians thrashing out trade agreements in some old parliamentary building. I was involved in one of these scenarios throughout my career, but the reality is that everybody has to take on a certain level of negotiation on a daily basis in regular civilian life. Whether it's negotiating for your child to eat those last two mouthfuls of dinner or getting that pay rise at work. You will be indulging in these types of interactions whether you know it or not, so you may as well sharpen your talking tools ready for when they do arise. In general, effective negotiation is just about doing 2 things in any situation:

1. Learning the high level negotiation strategies in preparation for these situations.

2. Implementing the correct behavior patterns to effectively pull them off in the moment.

In my previous book "Persuasion: An Ex-SPY's Guide" I laid out some of the key persuasion and conversational strategies for getting people round to your way of thinking. The techniques and strategies are very subtle and elegant and are intended for you to put into action on a daily basis in more regular discourse. A way of massaging conversations with your colleagues or spouse for a more positive outcome in your favour.

I was tempted to combine the two, negotiation and persuasion into one book but after writing the initial few chapters on each, I decided that they were unique enough and the differences significant enough to warrant a closer more individual scrutiny of each.

So having described the slightly more mellow persuasion tactics already, there are times in life, during some of the more critical moments where the stakes are higher and where a more measured and serious approach is required. This again doesn't imply that you have to use malicious or manipulating tactics, but more of an outcome orientated stance and emphasis on instant and tangible results. This is where proper negotiation comes in.

These moments will include the discussions of a salary rise or promotion at work, closing an important deal or simply buying that new car or house. These are the instances where you definitely need a greater level of preparation and help if you want the best possible outcome for yourself. Again this isn't about screwing over the other party, it's just about getting the best deal you can from what's available. If you happen to be a lawyer or work in investment banking then you might find your day-to-day is already filled with these types of interactions so it would be wise to pay very close attention. My life in the field with the CIA certainly had its fair share of critical negotiations, from cutting narcotics deals with crime bosses whilst undercover to securing key intelligence agreements with informants. I had to strategically plan out these interactions and employ the tactics you will learn in the following chapters to make sure I came out ahead. The stakes could not have been any higher.

I will lay out the strategies for effective negotiation however like anything you are attempting to become competent at in life, it will take a lot of practice and trial and error to master fully. I can provide you with some tips and tricks to get you started but it will take years of learning and adjusting as you go and as I always say, fail big and often when the stakes aren't necessarily that high to get you ready for the times when they are. So you might as well start now.

My Back Story

As with all of the subjects I have previously written on, you may be thinking, "Who is this guy that he is such an expert in negotiation? Why should I listen to him?" That's an important question, so here is what you need to know about me.

Firstly, I want you to think about everything you have ever learned about spies from the movies. Think about action-packed scenes, dangerous surveillance, and anything else you have learned from Hollywood. Now, take these preconceived notions and toss them out the window. Real spy work is not indiscriminate violence and high speed chases. Real spy work is usually done from afar; it's about getting things done with minimal fuss and without provocation. It's quiet and unassuming data gathering for the most part.

You'd also be surprised to find that spy work isn't necessarily gadgets and gizmos that do your work for you. Most of the time, it comes down to human psychological skills and the ability to improvise in any situation. And these skills can be developed and learned with a little practice.

I have to skip over some of the more specific details, as almost everything I have done over the past two decades is classified. Real names will be omitted as I detail some of my jobs and experiences around the world for the same reason.

I got my start in 1994 working a desk job for the FBI in my home state of Virginia. About a decade into my stint with them, my parents died in a car accident in our home town whilst sliding on an icy road into oncoming traffic one winter. Since it was my ties to my family that had kept me at home all these years, I decided to become a field agent as I figured I'd get to see a fair deal more than I currently was paper pushing behind a desk in Richmond. The transition wasn't as smooth as I'd anticipated. But a little under nine months after undertaking the training, I was a fully fledged Special Agent in the FBI. It took me all across the country, initially shadowing more experienced agents on white collar fraud cases but I soon graduated onto much more interesting work.

I have to confess that I did not know how good I would be at first. Everything that I had done in life up to this point though, I had succeeded at. From top grades in high school to the football scholarship at Florida State that I used to study forensics and psychology, I had succeeded in pretty much everything I'd tried. Regardless of why, I was good.

The FBI took note of this as they put me on more dangerous assignments as an undercover agent. I infiltrated criminal organizations and helped to take down illegal rackets of all descriptions. Sex, drugs, you name it. Eventually, I ended up on a case with another agent, an American spy. It was through him that I met my latest employer.

So, why am I an expert in negotiation? I have since left the CIA, but after many years working with the organization I had acquired a number of unique skill sets, counterintelligence, hand-to-hand combat, lock picking, body language analysis just to name a few. However, the ability to negotiate successfully in a range of situations was a big a part of my day-to-day for obvious reasons.

In my professional career I was both formally trained in negotiation and conflict resolution during my years with the FBI and then with more hands on experience in the field as a CIA intelligence operative. This started with low level gang disputes in our inner cities and leading onto the highest level hostage negotiations where the margin for error was nonexistent.

So now that you know my qualifications and what I bring to the table, let's dive in. The following chapters will teach you everything that you need to become a proficient negotiator, especially in those critical moments that matter most. Don't worry, I will provide plenty of stories about my work in the field (as well as real life scenarios that could apply to you) along the way to keep things interesting. But ultimately provide you with the tools and knowledge on how to negotiate your way to a better outcome in any situation.

PART 1

A BASIC UNDERSTANDING OF
NEGOTIATION PRINCIPLES

CHAPTER 1

A BRIEF HISTORY OF NEGOTIATION

"Negotiation and discussion are the greatest weapons
we have for promoting peace and development"

(Nelson Mandela)

The Evolution of Negotiation throughout History

When I first joined the bureau we were required to look back and study some of the general principles of human negotiation throughout history during my training, it was like induction level stuff with the FBI. The idea was that if you can have a look at where we have come from you can better understand the strategies of today, and even where we might be going with it. I have summarized the main points below for the same reason. It is thought that there are five general stages that are distinct from one another which have progressed alongside human civilization. A lot of this is connected to conflict and war in the early stages and then due to more collaborative efforts later on.

#1 Primal Negotiation

In early human history where war and conflict was pretty much a daily constant, a more primal form of negotiation existed. There were no centralized forms of government and somewhat of an "all against all" mentality between tribes. These early forms of negotiation at this time where more rudimentary and thought to reflect more closely with the fight resolution behaviors between animals, more instinctive in nature. However as the complexities of war and human civilization progressed in general, negotiation strategies also progressed alongside it.

Some of the earliest recorded Greek writings depict not only the nature of the war strategies during the Peloponnesian conflict between the Spartans and the Athenians, but also their efforts to mediate and negotiate the eventual truce. Military commanders and generals are actually credited for contributing many of the important developments in negotiation strategies over these early centuries and rightly so.

#2 Strategic Negotiation

This type of negotiation was proliferated largely due to the expanding nature of trade and inter-city wars of the Renaissance era during the 16th century. The greater requirement for critical thinking and intentional planning was required not only due to the Catholic Church initiating wars against other Italian states, but also foreign nations who were also maneuvering for power and control.

With a continuously shifting landscape of alliances the ability to predict and counteract, often in a very Machiavellian fashion, became of paramount importance. Again the theories and strategies of war advanced once more as well as the negotiation tactics alongside them.

#3 Early Rationalist Approach

Following on from the strategic era, the 17th and 18th centuries ushered in a more rational approach to negotiation as a result of the scientific revolution and enlightenment periods. The study of everything from physical materials, human anatomy and physiology, political and social sciences all advanced the thinking and reasoning capabilities of the time. This is when negotiation practices where starting to be viewed as a more rational and pragmatic endeavor as well.

It all began with thinkers and mathematicians like Rene' Descartes who wrote the famous phrase "cogito ergo sum," or more commonly known as "I think therefore I am," and stretched into the Newtonian discoveries of the late 1600's and all the way to the early 20th century before the start of the First World War.

#4 Technological Rational Negotiation

By the middle of the 20th century and following the Second World

War, the world was brimming with new technological advances but also beset by a new danger. Hiroshima and Nagasaki had shown the world what atomic weaponry could do and that there was a real and impending threat of nuclear war on this horizon.

The earlier more rational modes of negotiation started to become heavily scrutinized and made into more of a science within the military to negotiate the cold war. The elements of Game Theory and its strategic derivatives was the order of the day. These modern day strategies also started to become more industrialized and found their way into our workplaces as employment and business contracts were now abundant.

#5 Post-Modern Negotiation

The fifth and final stage of historical negotiation is what we have entered into today, an approach born out of the neuroscience and cognitive psychological studies throughout the later parts of the 20th century and the early 21st. The theories of today are based heavily on unpredictability and the irrationality human decision making.

We now live in a very complex time and our interactions reflect that. The world is a very high speed and interconnected place where tensions can arise often and quickly as a result. The more rational and linear problem solving standards of the past are somewhat insufficient to deal with the complex socioeconomic and geopolitical systems we have today.

This is where things started to get interesting for me, when I began studying these new human psychological negotiation tactics and ones that I would later put into practice for myself working for the CIA.

Modern Day Methods

Negotiation and reasoning are what make us thrive as a species and separates us from the rest of the animal kingdom by and large. Although you can observe empathetic and even collaborative behavior amongst animals, full scale cognitive negotiation seems to be reserved for us. Not least due to the fact we have advanced language faculties but also as we have a greater perceptual grasp of time, the ramifications of our past and future events.

Negotiation processes are required in all subsets of our lives where disagreement and disputes may arise. Everything from politics to law making, educational reform to environmental policy. All of these areas require a set of rules, guidelines and policies to follow and skilled and flexible people to mediate and evolve these systems over time.

However unless it is you job to perform in one of the sectors I mentioned above, then the most important area for most people to sharpen their negotiation skills is within their own personal and professional life. Within the interactions they face on a daily basis. Negotiations that will advance their professional prospects and improve their social relationships with friends and family alike. That's why it's critical to look at negotiation styles on a more personal level and what I will be focusing on from here on out.

BATNA

When it comes to negotiation theory there is usually the requirement for baselines and guidelines to be set to begin with. Harvard's Roger Fisher and William Ury were two members of the Universities Program of Negotiation (PON) who tried to do just that. Best Alternative to a Negotiated Agreement or BATNA is designed to describe the most adventurous alternative if a specific negotiation comes to a deadlock and an agreeable outcome cannot be made. Think of it like a dog leash, it can only be stretched so far.

BATNA is this leash for a negotiator, a kind of yard stick and reference framework that all successful negotiators should fall back on. It is the accepted norm that a person or group should typically not accept a less favorable outcome than their BATNA. Well that's the theory...

An example might be this. You are selling your house and you have been made an offer of $800,000 which will also be your BATNA as it has already been agreed upon. In reality, whilst having this framework is prudent in almost all cases of negotiation and arbitration, real life interactions are much more nuanced and convoluted. BATNA will work for the factual negotiator (described in greater detail in the following chapter) in more legislative and corporate settings. But for the relational everyday negotiations this frame work can be stifling. In reality, assessing your own and the other parties concrete options is difficult and the landscape of possible options always shifting. You may feel you are getting to far away from your agreed upon BATNA and forego an offer that otherwise would have had a bigger payoff than expected when more time to evaluate was taken.

Continuing on from the example above when selling the house, evaluating other qualitative factors can be difficult. Say you get an offer from a relative or close friend for $775,000 or even a cash offer for $750,000? What happens if you get an offer for $850,000 but the buyers can only put through the deal in 5 months time?

I don't want to bore you with the other various negotiation and conflict resolution principles/acronyms as in truth, whilst laying down the foundation to this field they are now largely outdated. The trend now is to take a much more human approach (compared to the previous more methodical and robotic approaches) where negotiators were more concerned with ticking off an escalating checklist rather than dealing with the true nature of the situation at hand. The strategies that work today are much more encompassing of irrational humans and their emotions that are equally likely to have gotten them into the standoff in the first place. So the next chapters are focused on exactly that.

CHAPTER 2

THE THREE NEGOTIATOR PERSONALITY PROFILES

Before we start to look at the specific strategies and tactics for successful negotiations, it's helpful to have a look at the three general categories a person will fall into regarding them. In reality everybody will be a mixture of all of these three personality types however they will always lean more heavily to one part in particular.

Type One: The Factual Negotiator

This person is largely concerned with the facts and figures and will ask exclusively factually related questions. They are there to cross the T's and dot the I's and are more common in legislative departments within corporations and often come from a background in law or retail banking.

The problem with these types of negotiators is that they are very cut and dry and as a result leave very little room for emotional connection and relational discourse. This can sometimes lead to more tense and uneasy exchanges with competing departments or companies especially if there are no type two negotiators on hand

111

to smooth things over.

Type Two: The Relational Negotiator

The second type of negotiator you will come across is the one I would most likely compare myself to. The relational negotiator does what their title suggests, they build relationships and trust with the other party through many of the conversational and empathy building tactics described in this book.

These types of negotiators are always looking to find connections and common ground and cultivate the most fertile environment for deals to be made and agreements struck. However this can also be their downfall, as they are often overly occupied with building trust and can lose sight of specifics tasks at hand.

Type Three: The Intuitive Negotiator

The third and final type is the intuitive negotiator. These people possess a more innate ability to interpret situations in the moment, they often go in with a plan but are happy to feel out the initial exchanges and adopt their style accordingly. These people are more similar to type two negotiators in the sense that they are looking to build a connection and mirror mannerisms where necessary.

The only problem that type three negotiators can encounter is one of ill discipline. They can have the propensity to go off in a certain direction, and similar to type two negotiators, can often get off track

So it's fairly important for you to know where you predominantly stand across these three negotiator personality types so you best know where your strengths lie and in turn are able to play to them. This will become more apparent in the following chapters when collaborative negotiation is an option and knowing where you would fit into a team effort on it.

The ideal and most well rounded negotiator will obviously be a perfect mix of all three types, a balanced individual who can adapt to any stylistic negotiation environment in which they find themselves in. Although I leaned more heavily toward the relational negotiation type, in truth I practiced the other two skill sets to a point that I knew that I could handle any situation that may arise and I developed a taste for when it was optimal to implement one style over another. You have to wear many hats working in the intelligence game for the CIA but in reality the person who can develop these three abilities in everyday life will also gain a big leg up when it comes to negotiating time.

CHAPTER 3

LAYING THE FOUNDATION FOR PRODUCTIVE TALKS

As with just about everything in life, being well prepared for whatever you are about to attempt will almost always give you the edge you need to win in that situation. In some instances it's absolutely key to your success and high stakes negotiation is no exception. Here are some of the elements to keep in mind before you dive in.

Cultivating an Empathetic Environment

As I mentioned in the previous chapter, today's negotiation strategies are more about taking emotions into account. If we follow the old rules of negotiation we would hold our cards very close to our chest in an attempt to not give anything away. If you think about it, that only tends to foster an environment of tension and distrust. We will explore the specific strategies on how best to avoid this later in the book but suffice to say for now, being more open with your information and options is a good thing.

I'm not saying reveal everything about yourself and laying all of your cards on the table, rather just allude to tidbits of information about your hobbies or personal life that are harmless yet sets a friendly and positive context for the discussion that is about to unfold. The other party is extremely likely to follow suit and will be much more open to the more valuable exchanges you are about to have as they are emotionally invested in your personality, even if it's in the smallest way.

Prioritize Your Outcomes

Before entering any form of discussion or negotiation it is always a good idea to rank or sequence the objectives you are looking to get from the exchange. I'm not talking about adhering to a strict set of BATNA rules, but something to guide your opening exchanges.

This might be securing a certain price (buying or selling) it might be terms (more vacation or better working conditions). Whatever this may be, be sure to list these factors down and lay them on the table and get the counterparty to do the same. This way you can see where you both stand and what realistic concessions can be made. You will be surprised; often times you can strike a very quick and favorable deal by being this transparent especially if everybody is on the same page with what they want.

Know Your Target Terms and Walk Away Price

So following on from this point, there is really two vitally important components to know before entering into any negotiation. That is the target terms you are shooting for and also your 'reservation value' which is simply the lowest possible price you would accept before walking away. Auctioneers always know this point and you should too whether you are selling a house or making concessions on a new job contract. Know your limits beforehand and leave with a calm head if it gets triggered.

You need to have fully researched these variables beforehand and be comfortable with each in advance. You are much more likely to rationally appraise these elements in the comfort of your own space when you are not in the heat of the moment discussion or negotiation on them. Especially if you are just on your journey to becoming a skilled negotiator and haven't mastered the behavioral traits and mannerisms conducive for high level negotiation described later on in this book.

So prepare your target price in advance and equally importantly the terms by which you would have to walk away. This will lead to a much more productive discussion and one in which you will be much less disappointed with if you do have to walk away as you've fully familiarized yourself with the outcomes beforehand. I had to back down from negotiations many times in the field with the CIA and not always due to a monetary value. I always knew when to cut my losses and so should you.

CHAPTER 4

THE IMPORTANCE OF VERBAL & NONVERBAL RAPPORT BUILDING

When it comes to communication in general, it is no secret that I believe that a relational communicator is the most effective personality type for effective persuasion and negotiation. It is important to come to the same level as the other person in order to really cultivate an environment that is most conducive to open and productive discourse. When tempers rise, barriers rise and the chances of persuading anybody of anything becomes almost impossible.

In this chapter, we will look at ways in which to build rapport, empathy and talk to someone on their level.

Rapport building in general simply means establishing an understanding with another person producing a harmonious environment; you are trying to point out similarities in your circumstances. This helps with building trust and bridging communication gaps. Good rapport can help with getting so much more out of people and the interactions you are having with them. It can assist with improving everything in your day-to-day living and make it easier to drive across important messages as a result. I spent so much time cultivating these types of relationships with other field agents and informants alike. Building rapport and empathy towards your position was like a social currency on the streets, you never know when you might have to cash it in.

There are two main ways in which one can build rapport with their and they are verbal and nonverbal. I will point out some specific strategies for doing these elements within a later chapter concerning mirroring mannerisms, but here are the overarching principles to note for now.

Verbal Rapport Building

Verbal rapport building simply refers to using your vocal skills to help develop this bond. As you know, it is extremely important to make use of your communication skills at every opportunity in order to understand another person and build that connection, and using your voice as a tool is a critical component. Here are some ways in which you can use it to your benefit.

General Language

A lot can be expressed via the human voice, we seem to be the only species that has developed the complex structures in the larynx, like the vocal chords etc to successfully produce language. Other species can certainly produce complex and intelligent sounds to communicate just fine and some like the parrot and even the beluga whale can mimic human speech to some extent. However none can actually articulate conversation like we can.

It's not only having the ability to talk that is the only benefit either, it equally comes down to the actual words and phrases we choose to speak. When attempting to build rapport with another person it's important to assess how they are speaking, it will pay to mirror this with your own lexicon so that you are striking a balance and demonstrating that you are both on the same level to some degree. If they are using rudimentary vocabulary then ensure that you make use of simple language yourself that is free from ambiguity. If however they are using a greater range of diction, then attempt to adjust yours to match it accordingly.

It is also a good idea to mirror the persons talking rhythms as well as the type of language they are using. You will find that you do this naturally to some degree but make sure you are aligning the pitch, tone and intonations to your voice, matching it with theirs. Again this helps with bringing a harmony and rhythm to the interaction that will indicate that both parties have more similarities than differences and can be trusted by one another as a result.

Listening Skills

I talk about the importance of being a great listener extensively in

"Persuasion: An Ex-SPY's guide" but it is of equal relevance here. Remember that people make it more complicated than it has to be at times, I promise you, if you truly listen to what somebody is saying you will know what they are thinking. Very few people can truly mask what's in their thoughts with what they are saying, it's harder than you think and I was trained to spot this happening.

The vast majority of people in everyday civilian life will be as forthcoming as can be, so pay attention and listen to what they are saying when they speak. In order to establish a good rapport, you have to listen to the other person carefully. Don't make it all about you even if you have a lot of input to give. You must give the other person a fair chance to speak and really hear what they are saying as opposed to just waiting for your turn to talk. Listen with a keen ear and make the person speaking comfortable. It will help you identify more topics to talk about and reduce the communication gap. Indulge in active listening where you listen with full attention before deciding on what your next move will be.

Also it goes without saying that if you really want to hear what the other person is saying then you will need to interrupt them as little as possible. Only do so when it's absolutely necessary as often times interrupting someone will ensure they lose the train of thought and can move you away from the topic at hand. Let the other person finish their passage before adding your inputs. Make a mental note of your thoughts and start addressing the points one by one as soon as the other person stops speaking.

Humor

One of the best tools to use while trying to build rapport is humor. Humor can help you connect on a deeper level as you will again demonstrate the commonalities in your personalities and that you view the world in much the same way. This obviously takes some innate skill or intentional practice but developing an ability to draw comedic and satirical value from situations and stories will be a very worthwhile endeavor.

Try to make the interaction as light and jovial as possible so that you have the chance to build that connection and common ground. Bring out relevant topics and make jokes pertaining to the conversation. Everyone likes to moan about their favorite sports team or the state of the weather so use this small talk to your advantage. But remember to always keep it light and nothing personal.

Honesty

As well as injecting some humor into the initial conversations and exchanges, also be open and honest with the other person when you wish to build a rapport. As I have previously stated in my opening remarks about building an empathetic environment, allude to tidbits of information about your hobbies or personal life that are harmless enough yet sets a friendly and positive context for the discussion.

People tend to reciprocate behavior so divulging something trivial about yourself will help build that initial trust and in turn will encourage the other party to do the same. Always try to reserve any judgment of opinion as your intention here is not to try and win a discussion, but merely to cultivate the environment for a positive one to take place. Once they are comfortable confiding in the small things you can slowly start to turn it up a notch.

Nonverbal Rapport Building

Apart from verbally establishing a rapport, you must compliment that effort and also work towards establishing a nonverbal connection by using your movements and gestures. Here are the different aspects to bear in mind.

Posture

Always try to maintain the correct posture when trying to build a rapport. Firstly, it's a good idea to lean in towards the person ever so slightly when listening to them which is an authentic gesture to show that they know you are genuinely interested in what they have to say. But always maintain a straight posture while listening and/or talking and try to make enough eye contact to ensure they feel important and engaged but not uncomfortable.

Keep your hands free from pockets and in sight. Place them on the table if there is one with palms faced down. This is a neutral position and shows that you are solely focused on conversing and nothing else. I alluded to this story in a previous book but as a spy you are always concerned with what someone is doing with their hands. Hands are used to fire weapons and throw punches, if somebody hides them then it's almost always trouble. Of course in settings such as these I wouldn't expect anybody to try anything like that, but showing your hands allows the other person to relax and subconsciously feel at ease.

Gestures

Along the similar lines as the above, make use of the gestures you are using to complete the rapport building effort. Your movements should again be as neutral as possible, non-threatening and mimicking the other person which further builds rhythm and harmony to the connection. Most of these things will actually be subconscious cues to a large extent but highly important none the less. Like subtle facial expressions such as raising an eyebrow or scratching of the head/neck to clenching of the hands. These things will be picked up on even though they may seem insignificant. Others will be more overt and intentional like mimicking rocking in a chair, larger arm movements and reciprocating laughter.

You must try to reciprocate everything here to show the other person that you are interested and engaged in what they are saying to build that mutual rapport. It's also never a bad idea to try and elicit a happier mood which can be done as easily as maintaining a smile when they other person is talking as it encourages them to open up even more. Uoo enthusiastic expressions when speaking so that they better take to what you are saying and are likely to respond more positively as a result. But remember never to be restless. If the previous advice was designed to build that smooth and harmonious rapport, the one thing that can undue all of that is a restless and fidgety persona. So avoid it at all costs.

PART 2

HIGH LEVEL NEGOTIATION STRATEGIES & BEHAVIORAL TACTICS FOR THE REAL WORLD

CHAPTER 5

CLEVER PSYCHOLOGICAL BUYER/SELLER NEGOTIATION TRICKS

"In business as in life, you don't get what you deserve,
you get what you negotiate"

(Chester L. Karrass)

You quickly workout in the field as a spy and in life in general that certain skills and abilities are universal and actually critical to success. I wouldn't class myself as a sales person per se, but I did develop a very proficient level of skill for it. Regardless of what you do in life you will always be selling something, even if it's your own skills and abilities. And of course you can never fully avoid buying/selling things, especially when it becomes time to purchase that new car or sell the house.

The following principles are techniques that were trained into me during my time with the FBI. They are important psychological tricks to understand even if you are not involved in a sales position because as I mention, you will always be on the buyer or seller side of something sooner or later.

The Boulwarism Approach

Boulwarism is a negotiation tactic that got its name from General Electric's former vice president Lemuel Boulware who essentially pioneered the strategy. It comes from the many labor law disputes he had with the various unions at the time. It's actually meant to be a more final offer, a kind of "take it or leave it" kind of deal.

However if you do not want to be quite as final in your approach you can always opt for a slightly softer variation of the "all I have" tactic. The basic premise of this strategy is to overtly state that "this is all I have" early on in the negotiation. It's a basic scarcity tactic. The idea is to clarify a budget that is 20-30% lower than the current asking price and stick with it. This strategy is most commonly used when buying an expensive item like a car or house although equally applies to the smaller stuff. Stating a finite figure upfront will set a ceiling in the sellers mind and start the process of them finding concessions to get down to that price. This is especially true if you evoke some level of empathy or even sympathy within the person regarding your position.

However as with the Boulwarism approach, this can be a high risk strategy as you are basically setting a final offer upfront which won't always be a successful tactic. Especially if whatever you are buying is in high demand as the dealer can just hold out for other buyers who are willing to pay the full list price. However if you can do your research beforehand to indentify these circumstances in advance, it can be a very successful approach.

Trial Ballooning

This is a tactic that's often referred to as 'trial closing' in sales. It's a starting point and equally relevant whether you are on the seller or the buying side of a negotiation. The idea is to start out with the final solution, a tentative offer made that you had in mind. So just put it out there and see if the balloon flies. Do not be afraid to go big out of the gate. Making the first offer in any exchange usually puts you in a worse position as you've shown your cards, which is why it's imperative to go bold. An aggressive offer will 'anchor' the price point at a high one even though the other party will almost always bring you down from there, you will still be in a better position overall. And you never know they may accept this trial balloon straight off the bat especially if they are in a hurry to get a resolution.

Open with statements like "If we can come to an agreement on XYZ, then can we close this thing right now?" As I mentioned above, it's much more likely that these types of suggestions will be questioned and opposed initially but you can now at least find a way down to some more common ground that should be at a higher level in your favor.

Auction Model

This strategy can only be put into play when there are multiple buyers at the table. It is simply the action of playing one party off against another in order to create a buying frenzy and drive up the price for whatever you are selling.

Humans are naturally competitive creatures and when faced with opposition to something they want, often can drive very primitive instincts to acquire whatever it is that's on the table. Possession seems to be an innate need for us especially if we haven't rationally appraised the real use for it beforehand making exponential bidding wars almost inevitable.

I once witnessed a deal being brokered between two of the most prominent African dictators at the time. Initially they were at the meeting on separate business however both were looking to purchase some more state of the art weaponry that would improve their respective arsenals. However the broker who had set up the meeting, who also happened to be the biggest arms dealer in the southern hemisphere, had them both sit in on the same session as his time was extremely limited.

After dictator number one had finalized his business with some automatic firearms and a handful of T-90 Russian tanks, he sat back and observed the dealer present the real prize to dictator number two. They were a set on remotely controlled Reaper Drone's that were a slightly earlier version than the MQ9's used today. They could fly high altitude missions and deliver significant payloads all from a computer screen thousands of miles away.

"Eh, how come you never offered these ones to me?" the first guy shouted in a heavy African accent. What followed was a series of offers and counter offers each higher than the last for the set of drones on sale. Now without knowing this for sure, I'm almost certain that the arms dealer who had set up the meeting, did so in a way that he knew these two chaps would inevitably enter into the bidding war (for want of a better term) that rather quickly ensued.

Now this is obviously quite a dramatic example of an auction style negotiation in action. But in everyday life it is also your job to bring two parties of buyers together when the time calls for it, albeit in much more amicable settings than the one I mentioned above. Still it's up to you to subtly nudge them into this process and let them get on with it by themselves. Let each person be aware of what the other is offering and let them do the rest.

Offer Biasing

This is a tactic you can often use when you have a variance of options you can offer. You will initiate the discussion by putting on the table seemingly mutual and neutral options; however these will in fact be moderately or heavily biased in your favor. The idea is to present a set of options that if any choice is taken it will be preferable to you. Try to elegantly remove anything that would not be of interest and instead offer a selection that will naturally lead into the options most agreeable to you.

Everybody has these natural biases they lean towards and a good negotiation strategy is to play to these biases buy adding and removing options in the most professional way possible. This isn't the entirely underhand or deceiving tactic as it may sound, the other party can always decline and add to additional options if they see fit. But framing the choices beforehand can really set the scene in your favor to begin with. It's much like setting the "All I have" price I mentioned above and anchoring a set of objectives to begin with.

This often works very well in more relaxed settings with family and friends. Try suggesting two movies to friends that you would really prefer to go and see and subtly add in a third that you don't, but with the caveat that it wasn't received well at film festivals. You've already set the tone for what everybody is likely to pick! Real estate agents also employ this tactic when showing new prospects properties, they will bring them to view two properties initially which are just outside a buyers price range before showing them a third that is within their budget but highly unsuitable. The buyers are obviously still free to make any choice they wish, however will start to justify the higher priced houses in their head based on the biased choices they were given.

Russian Front

Another choice or decision based negotiation strategy you can employ if you have a certain degree of control in a selling situation is the 'Russian Front' method. It's an expression that originated from World War II in Nazi Germany when the fighting began on the Eastern front between European Axis powers and the Soviet Union. It was one of the largest and most brutal conflict zones in history and one where you were just as likely to be killed from the cold as you were from a Russian bullet. The German soldiers hated going there and for good reason.

The idea with this strategy is to paint a very grim picture of the initial option you are offering, one that is clearly undesirable and will cause the person unease and discomfort and ultimately will never choose. You then follow this up with the second option or offer which is a hugely more desirable one, a kind of olive branch from the first. If you are trying to sell somebody on a job you would like them to take, you might say something like "I know there are positions down in the warehouse as the folk lift truck hospitalized two guys recently but I'm sure you'll be fine. On the other hand I do have contacts up here in head office too… should I speak with them on your behalf?"

This is done all of the time in criminal and law enforcement negotiations and interrogations. The accused suspect will regularly be painted the picture of long jail time and harsh treatment before being offered the plea deal in exchange for more favorable terms. Granted these guys have much less room to maneuver compared to everyday and professional negotiations, but it illustrates the point very well none the less.

Thought Pattern Interrupts

I have written about this principle in previous books but one of the most important things you are taught when working for the CIA is to identify baselines and standards of behavior in every and all situations. This allows you to much more quickly identify when something is amiss. Negotiation is no different, the trick is to identify what benchmarks somebody has constructed in their minds and see if you can disrupt that line of thinking where possible.

You will have to ask them a battery of baseline questions to begin with to establish these cognitive norms but it will be well worth the effort. Get the person to describe their ideal outlook on whatever you are negotiating and how they would see it going perfectly. I always found that being upbeat with this process ensured the person would give up a greater amount as that would put them in a much more conducive state for it. Then it's your job to change the outlook on these standards if they do not meet your own objectives.

Car salesmen will often ask you what you are ideally looking for in a new vehicle, they are searching for norms in your thinking based on your belief systems about cars and more importantly, what you find attractive about the one you are potentially about to buy. If you suggest that you like family four door saloons as they are fuel efficient and spacious enough for your family to fit inside, he may change this standard for you by detailing the equally fuel efficient, yet more spacious SUV with even greater safety features for just a few extra thousand dollars. It's kind of a bait and switch for you mind.

Now I'm not saying that the above is necessarily false, the more expensive car may in fact be a better deal or it may not. The point though is this, we make these contrasting comparisons all of the time and that it is your job to shift these paradigms in thinking in your favor when it comes to negotiating whatever you have on the table.

Always Offer a Range

This one is another psychological trick you can employ but this time when you are on the selling side or offer side. Research has found that when demanding a single digit figure whilst negotiating the price for something, this almost never works as well as offering a range. For example, if you are trying to sell somebody an apartment and you would like to receive $500,000 for it. Offer $500,000 to $550,000 as the asking price.

This is often referred to as a "bolstering range". Now you could say, why not just offer $550,000 and let the buyers naturally barter you down to $500,000 anyway .However it's all about perception, offering the range upfront shows that you are much more reasonable from the outset and more likely to avoid the aggressive counter offers that may follow. People will feel much more obliged to offer somewhere within that range to reciprocate the perceived fairness and goodwill shown to them.

It's actually even more relevant when you are demanding or asking for something for yourself such as a salary negotiation. If you believe you are worth $80,000 per year, then instead ask for $80,000 to $100,000. Again, this makes you seem reasonable in your offer and things are likely to be much more amicable as a result. You are also upward adjusting your boss's valuation of your worth and who knows, they may even offer to meet you half way.

Sell Your Potential, Not Your Skills

Lastly I wanted to include a strategy you can use for when you need to sell yourself. This can be in a job interview, relationship, anything where you need to convince the other person to give you a shot. Most people spend their time in these types of personal selling situations by reeling off all of their prior accomplishments and current skill sets. However whilst mentioning these things is of course prudent and necessary to do so, they are not the factors in which you should actually be focusing most of your effort on. You need to be more concerned with emphasizing your potential than anything else.

"The first principle of contract negotiation is not to remind them what you did in the past; tell them what you are going to do in the future."

(Stan Musial)

A recent Stanford-Harvard study found evidence for the theory that a person's accomplishments aren't what really capture another person's attention, but rather the person's perceived potential. The ambiguous and uncertain nature that is inherent with potential appears to be much more cognitively engaging compared to simply reflecting on what is already established and known to be true.

As I mentioned, most people spend all of their time laboriously regurgitating their past job spec's and responsibilities from their CV. What they are intending to do in the future is just an afterthought. Whilst I do agree that citing specific instances where you ran into an issue or were met with a challenge and then stating the steps you took to overcome it is definitely a beneficial tactic.

Problem solving and critical thinking are a big plus for employers these days as just about every white collar job requires it. Machines and AI are putting pay to the more menial and repetitive robotic work at a frightening pace. I haven't worked a regular job since I was in high school but it's not difficult to notice the trends even from the outside. So the next time you are trying to convince somebody of your own worthiness, focus on what you are going to bring them in the future, not what you brought others in the past.

CHAPTER 6

NEGOTIATION STRATEGIES & TACTICS FOR THE BOARDROOM/ BUSINESS & BEYOND

As I mentioned in the opening remarks to this book, there are some over arching negotiation principles that it would be wise to study in preparation for the crucial events in life. The strategies which follow are a compilation of what I have studied and put into practice to great effect during my time as an FBI special agent and CIA field operative.

However the tactics you will learn here are equally effective and applicable to everyday negations and especially those in the professional workplace and business life. Although the stakes can often be high, it's important to not take this stuff to seriously where the one-upmanship style exchanges can be seen as more of a game at times. One that you can master and win if practiced in the right way and in the right spirit.

Logrolling

'Logrolling' is a practice that is performed on a daily basis in many high level positions and none more so than within politics. It's the practice of exchanging favors, especially if they are low priority concessions that can be made without a great level of consequence to the person doing the conceding. A game of 'quid pro quo' if you like, one that is especially common when it comes to legislation voting within parliamentary houses all around the globe.

I indulged in my fair share of this behavior during my time with both the FBI and CIA where it becomes a kind of currency not only in office politics but more importantly in the field too. But it's also a very powerful strategy within a negotiation, especially if you play your cards right. The idea is to propose a plethora of requests to the other side, some of very high importance but more crucially many that are not. This will allow you the ability to maneuver and to make, or be perceived to be making many concessions on things that were not hugely important to you in the first place. You can at least match the other person in terms of what they are prepared to let go. If done in a genuine fashion this will also help to build into the empathetic relationship you are trying to cultivate.

Switching Personnel

I alluded to a story in 'Confidence: An Ex-SPY's guide' in which I had to fill in for some guys that were called away whilst interviewing a suspect during my early time with the FBI. Granted it was more of an interrogation type of interaction rather than negotiation, but the principles still definitely apply. In truth this is more of a 'good cop bad cop' scenario you see in movies and on TV.

The theory is that by switching the person actually doing the negotiating, you can get a slightly different angle on the discussion that can hopefully push things in your favor. This works especially well if you have a friend or colleague who is adept in a different style of questioning or reasoning from you, who is of a different negotiating personality type I described previously. Try your way first and if you do not have any joy, then switch to your partner. If things are going really badly then the new negotiator can even start from scratch.

As I have suggested previously, positive negotiations or even interactions in general are built of f of emotional interaction between the humans involved. It can be a team game too. If you have the resources to have more than one negotiator on your team when sitting these sessions, then do it. You may find that your partner can strike a chord in the meeting but you cannot or vice versa. As with everything I suggest in this book, it's all about experimentation and practice.

Set the Agenda

Much like the offer biasing principle I described in the previous chapter, setting or controlling the agenda for a negotiation can be crucial in how the actual interaction plays out. The idea is that if you have control over the chronological order of items being discussed, you can better control the likely outcomes. You have to give good thought into how people will be feeling at any given point.

"Negotiation is a give and take process, but being in control of the process is the best way to be successful at it"

(Celso Cukierkorn)

It is advisable to put the more meaningless or indifferent items (for you) at the beginning of the discussion as everyone will be fresh and more easily able to dissect the topic at hand. You will find that these initial points of contention will either go your way or not, but if you have scheduled things correctly it shouldn't be of much consequence as they will be points that are neither here nor there for you.

The trick is to not use up a lot of mental energy dissecting them yourself, let the other party do that. Your intension will be to save this critical analyzing juice for the more important points (for you) later on in the discussion when the other side is tired and mentally fatigued. You do not want them to be thinking as clearly and they will likely be more willing to concede concessions purely based on the fact that they won't be thinking as sharply.

This is obviously only applicable when you have control of the meeting and agenda but you will need to be equally aware of these factors when you are not, and be ready to counteract them where you can. Conserving mental energy intelligently especially in long and drawn out negotiations can be vital to winning the points you need to. If things aren't going particularly well you may have to implement a pre-planned exit strategy. I list many of these within 'Confidence: An Ex-SPY's Guide' but they are not too difficult to come up with for yourself.

Buying Time

If you are unable to put any of your exist strategies into action then there is one thing you can try and that is intentional stalling or buying time when things are not going to plan for you. This can work in two ways; firstly it can get you out of a tight spot if you are feeling hurried or unsure of what you should be conceding in a negotiation. Secondly, it can also come in handy if you know the other side is constrained by a deadline and by delaying the time it takes to complete the discussion can mean them partially or fully conceding important points as a result.

Never be afraid to ask to be excused for a bathroom break where you can re-group your thoughts and also count down the clock to give added pressure to the other side. However buying time can be a much more covert process than leaving the room if you need it to be, which can sometimes anger the other side and do you more harm than good.

I was often in situations where it definitely wasn't possible to leave the table in complex negotiations undercover in the CIA, serious crime bosses do not allow it. In these instances I would simply labor a point that I had little interest in the outcome of whilst mulling over a more important one I knew would be later on the agenda. You have to be careful to do this in a tactful way in order to not heighten the tension excessively and to a point where it becomes counterproductive.

Again as with all of the tactics I describe in this book and others, the strategies can take years of experimentation and calibration to perfect. So try to practice buying a little time in your everyday interactions when the pressure isn't necessarily on, which will better prepare you for when it is.

Inside Man

As the name suggests, this tactic is one which is borrowed straight from the intelligence playbook itself. You will find that there are some instances where it is possible and indeed highly beneficial to elicit the help of an insider to help your negotiation cause.

During the early 2000's I was positioned for a number of years in southern Europe, I was actually the Portuguese station chief at the time. Several years prior to this I was located in Rio de Janeiro and Sao Paulo working the intelligence on drug cartels coming out of the Amazon in the north so was now fluent in the language. Although there are subtle differences between Brazilian compared to the native Portuguese dialect, they were similar enough for me to be able to handle the Lisbon post.

It was about a year into this stint when I was commissioned to bring an end to an organization that was siphoning off millions of Euros from the local stock exchange using a highly sophisticated algorithm running from machines so close to the exchange building that they could essentially arbitrage over 50 points a day across a variance of stocks and indices due to the speed of the quotes they were getting compared to the general market. In reality it was just a handful of very smart guys who were working the system, but they were causing a big enough splash for international markets to notice.

This is actually a gray area that many US quantitative and high frequency traders exploit to this day, but back then this type of trading was in its infancy and it was deemed to be highly illegal by the Europeans. It wasn't helped by the fact that it was affecting the stock price of some of the smaller US corporations along with some Asian commodities companies that we had a large vested interest in.

The problem was that the local law enforcement couldn't pin point exactly where this group had their machines positioned or ever gather enough evidence to prosecute them for what they were doing. It took me several months to figure it out myself but after noticing that these guys required a specific type of fiber optic cable to allow the super high speed computers and data feeds to function, I had an idea of how to get to them. I basically put a freeze on any local dealers supplying this cable within the city and made sure that I trained another operative, we'll call him 'Jake' who was in my team at the time to act as a freelance hardware supplier of the sort this organization needed.

Initially they were wary of my guy and closed down their operation for a couple of months in order to avoid detection but greed and impatience soon got the better of them. They eventually decided to enlist Jake's help in supplying them with the cable however the drop off points were always scattered around the city and never where their trading stations were positioned. It took just over 3 months for him to convince them to bring him onboard and a threat that he would stop supplying them with what they needed if they didn't. A little blackmail is never completely off the table in this game… They eventually agreed to the terms and got him to install the cable directly onto their computers near the exchange. Little did they know that Jake was actually downloading all of their trading data from a pen drive at one of their main sites. Needless to say this was enough to shut these guys down indefinitely.

Now I'm not saying that you have to go to these lengths to infiltrate an organization you are planning to negotiate with. But it illustrates my point. It could be that you befriend a colleague in another department to garner some information about their boss before sitting an important interview with him yourself. On the same note it's wise to be cognizant of anybody who is seemingly very eager and willing to help you out around the time of an important negotiation yourself as they could potentially by aiding your counterparty in much the same way as Jake was for me.

Sequential Conversion

This strategy is somewhat similar to the one stated above when enlisting other peoples help, but this time in a slightly different manner. The premise here is that when you need to win over a group of people with whom you are negotiating with, it's best to start with them one at a time. This will ultimately take more time to employ but will reap much more positive results for you if implemented with success.

The idea is that you can reasonably and easily convert one person to your way of thinking as you can deal with them on a much more personal level. You can employ any one of the empathy inducing tactics explained in this book and others. Then you can move sequentially and incrementally up the chain of opposition negotiators bringing them on board one at a time. If you do things correctly each of the people you positively convert should help in your efforts to convert the next and so on. This will have an aggregation affect that exponentially increases your efforts. You are building up a coalition of sorts

If you are negotiating with your organization as part of a team, then identify who would be in the most support of your interests and go after them in an intelligent manner until you have brought all on board. Do your homework and match the personality types of you team with those of the opposition to find the best fit and go from there.

Tactical Leaking

Information is definitely the most valuable commodity when it comes to any kind of negotiation. There is also a fine line between spying and the act of legitimate information gathering. Blurring the lines on this was obviously an occupational hazard for me. However there is another effective strategy when it comes to intel gathering which can be applied in the build up to an important negotiation, that is known as tactical leaking.

The information being "leaked" certainly doesn't have to be misleading information in anyway. It can be something that may well be accurate, but rather information you'd prefer the other side focuses on whilst distracting them from something more important. This strategy is also a lot more effective when the leaked information is perceived to be unintentional and unbeknown to the person or organization that let it slip. This should lead the other party, who are now privy to the intel, to believe they have the upper hand and gain a false sense of security of as a result.

Intelligence agencies and governments do this all of the time and it's got to the point where there are entire departments and processes both in field stations and at Langley which are solely dedicated to decipher whether the intel they have is in fact genuinely leaked or has been intentionally put into their hands by somebody who wants it to be there.

Regardless, leaking certain information strategically can be a very clever and useful tactic if utilized wisely. There are few things that are truly more beneficial than your counterparty in a negotiation exchange believing that they have some important intel on you and that they have the upper hand as a result. In reality, if you leaked it to them correctly they will be at a considerable disadvantage as you know that they are likely to be very focused on what you have fed to them and much less on some potentially more critical issues you can better prepare for.

It's obviously important to release this information as discretely as possible, often an overheard conversation, a corridor confession to a sympathetic ear under supposed confidentiality between work colleagues or business associates works the best. Or even documents left lying around where they shouldn't be. Have a think about what you have in your possession that could possibly find its way into the other side's hands the next time you face crunch talks or an important negotiation.

Off The Record

This strategy can be quite similar to the tactical leaking method I described above and can be combined very well in certain instances. They are both intended to let a certain amount of information pass to the other side that ordinarily would have been held back. They are also both usually performed leading up to and before the main and crucial negotiation session in a kind of preparation play.

This tactic is also commonly used by governments and political negotiators when an impasse has been reached and some level of "back-channeling" is required outside of the official discourse to help move things along.

However there are some subtle differences. Asking a person if you can go "off the record" or "speak in confidentiality" is a more direct way of handing them the information you would like them to hear, but still not in an official manner. You obviously won't be giving them anything you truly do not want to be brought up during your main negotiation meeting as you cannot be totally sure it will stay confidential. But it is a very good way to build that empathy yet again between the two sides. It's a show of trust and one that will be reciprocated if done correctly.

Most people will also use the "off the record" tactic to actually gain information for themselves. It's a game of give and take and feeling out what the other side is thinking. You can say "Look, this would obviously stay confidential but is Stephen actually contemplating accepting the offer or is he just stalling?" Again this is more of a feeling out process and although you are now engaging in an empathic exchange of trust, what they might be giving you may still be what they want you to hear. So it's important to look for vocal tone and visual cues in the person's body language to interpret if what they are saying is true or not. I will write more extensively on this within "Body Language: An Ex-SPY's guide". For now just go with your instincts and as always practice this method along with the others described in this chapter until you have a better grasp on it.

Whilst you can certainly read this chapter in under a day, it would be wise to go back and study each individual business negotiation principle and tactic individually and try to implement one at a time until you master its effects. These are rarely cut and dry techniques with a lot of nuanced variables that only become mastered with practice and time.

However, once you have got a number of the strategies down, you can then start to stack them one on top of another until you are habitually behaving like a top level negotiation strategist when it comes to thrashing out those boardroom and business deals. And remember to not take everything too seriously; it is after all just a game.

CHAPTER 7

A SPY'S TALKING TOOLS & BEHAVIORAL MODIFICATION TRICKS TO EXECUTE IN THE MOMENT

The strategies I described in the previous chapters where designed to get you thinking like a first class negotiating strategist. Negotiation in reality is just a simple extension of the intelligence game in general. It's like a game of chess, with the pieces of information being moved around the board in a carefully thought out manner.

However there is another element to successful negotiation that we haven't yet discussed. It's another layer, but this time one that more closely mirrors the game of poker. Where you have to make a series of affirmative action's but also react to those of your opponents in the moment. It's a game of reading emotional and behavioral patterns and adjusting yours accordingly. Most people can grasp the concepts and high level strategies I have already laid out, but many fall down when it comes to the execution of them as it takes a human skill set that you have either naturally developed or not. Thankfully with some guidance and practice these techniques can be learned and the following chapter will describe some of the most important tips and tricks to help you do just that.

Tip #1: Practice Situational Empathy

As I've stated on more than one occasion, the emotions of the human's involved in negotiation and conflict resolutions can't be ignored in the slightest. Human beings are emotional creatures and boiling things down to black and white never works, life is lived in the grey areas and none more so than in intense negotiations. The old school would suggest you should leave your emotions at the door when coming to the negotiating table. However in my many years of experience in persuading and negotiating with others, it's simply impossible to discount them fully, so planning and accounting for emotions will leave you in a much more realistic and ultimately more beneficial position.

I have already alluded to this empathy building process but one of the main components you need to start with is to let the other person know more about you than they currently do. This doesn't have to be anything especially intimate or even true, just something to do with your background or family that will endear you to the opposite side.

I always started off a negotiating conversation with some random fact and small talk about my day, "you know this sun/rain gets me every time". Everybody can relate to the weather. It is the universal ice breaker in any language; it puts people at ease as you have found some common ground no matter how mundane it is. It has been studied and showed that within business interactions the people who indulged this 'small talk' were 59% likely to come to an agreement whereas the people who kept it strictly business only secured one 40% of the time.

For me it was simply about getting a conversation off and running before moving onto the trickier stuff...

Tip #2: Mirror Mannerisms

So following on from that, once you have gotten some initial traction with your talks, it's time to employ another effective way to further increase this situational empathy which is to start to mirror the other person's mannerisms. You will find good talkers, listeners and negotiators alike will do this naturally. However you have to make sure that you do it intentionally and selectively. When you are mirroring another person's behavior they will pick up on this very quickly, more than likely subconsciously and start to mimic you back. Try to match the speed and vocal tone of their speech patterns. One of the techniques that worked for me very well was repeating the other person's words and grievances back to them especially within a hostage style standoff.

I was once trying to talk down a guy in a Chicago high-rise in my later years with the FBI. He was held up in his apartment with his youngest son and the reports were that he was holding a shotgun whilst refusing to let his wife in to take custody of his boy. It wasn't necessarily a cut and dry hostage situation as he hadn't intimated that he would not let his son go, just that he wouldn't let his wife in. Regardless things were more than tense and it was my job to talk him round.

In an attempt to see eye to eye with this guy I started to get into his head and ask him about his situation. This included repeating what he was saying back to him. I would say "your wife and kids are leaving you hey" I took a pause "you know my wife left me a few years ago too". I continued "it was hard, but this is how I dealt with it". Not only did the guy start to feel at ease that somebody understood his situation, I was also offering light at the end of the tunnel and that others have also gone through what he was and that it could be worked out. Having let me into the apartment by this point I also started to mimic his body language, posture, facial expressions and all forms of physical gestures. It took another couple of hours for him to agree to hand over the weapon and let us take him in, but when he did it was very calmly and quietly.

Mirroring a person's mannerisms and behavior patterns is done naturally in all of the best interactions between humans, and for good reason. It builds empathy and a bonding that makes both parties feel connected and at ease and much more likely to give concessions from their side. It has been observed time and again that negotiators who mimicked their opponent almost always secure a better outcome as a result.

Tip #3: Don't be afraid of "No"

If you follow many old school teachings on negotiation you will find that they would like you to escalate a line of questioning to get a "Yes" or an incremental ladder of "Yes's". The theory is that it puts the person in an agreeable state of mind and more likely to eventually come around to your way of thinking. However in reality this is often seen as an obvious attempt to manipulate the person into something they do not want to do, they anticipate this trap and usually break the line of questioning. An attorney would refer to this as 'cornering'.

"A "No" uttered from the deepest conviction is
better than a "Yes" merely uttered to please,
or even worse, to avoid trouble"

(Mahatma Gandhi)

When you are negotiating with a client or colleague ask questions that allow them to express their stance on the issue so they feel more secure and in control. Say something like "have your side completely rejected this proposal then?" This will give them the opportunity to decline and make them feel in control. It will also afford them a sense of security that will greatly smooth the path through the reminder of the negotiation if done correctly. So don't be afraid to get them to say "No".

Tip #4: The "I agree" Principle

I touched on this within the story above regarding the Chicago father but it's worth pointing out again. If you can really reaffirm and summarize a person's grievances and exactly how they are feeling about a certain situation, they pick up on this "I agree" moment you have given them. It has to be done in a genuine manner but when it is, the person feels that somebody else has also gone through what they have and that there is a solution for the problem. This is especially important within high stakes and emotional hostage negotiations but it is equally relevant for everyday and business settings.

The next time somebody states "I feel this deal is unfair to my client". Just reply with "I agree, lets figure out a way that we can get everybody to a favorable solution". This is really only a small sound bite on your part as you both were always going to contend the points at hand, but will have a big payoff in terms of the counterparty's emotional response. It again emphasizes a connection and reminds the person that you share empathy with their position and not just waiting for your turn to talk and state your point.

Try it the next time anybody gives you even the slightest objection to something, even if it's the way you made their coffee. Just say "I agree" and watch the reaction you get. The person's guard immediately drops as it's a surprising and counterintuitive thing for somebody to do so readily. It doesn't mean that you are backing down, just disarming the person of any psychological resistance to your next move/statement and initiate the urge within them to reciprocate in an agreeable way.

Tip #5: Challenge Requests with "Why's"

One of the most effective conversational weapons you have at your disposal is to be able to always ask "why?" You should always be challenging and contending points the other side is proposing and what it is exactly that are they suggesting. Ask "why are you requesting X?" and "why is it important for you to attain Y?" This line of questioning isn't intended to be done in an aggressive or interrogating fashion, but more of a probing and tactful way. Go up the sequence of questioning and challenge their reasoning to really establish the casual links to what they are saying and the consequences of that.

Much like the strategies I've already described above, this will also make the other side feel that they in control, that they are really being heard out as you are giving them the opportunity to carefully clarify their position. From my experience people really like to talk about themselves and their desires so lay a red carpet for them to be able to do it.

The two big benefits for you on this one is that you get to really understand what the other person is saying (not just making your own presumptions) and it's also a great way to get them to use up a lot of mental energy describing and dissecting their points. As I have described in an earlier principle, this can really work in your favor when a person starts to concede points or less likely to contend potentially more important ones later on in the discussion when they are mentally and physically fatigued. This is a tactic which is used in hostage negotiations all over the world. If you can talk for long enough and exhaust all the possible avenues in a person's mind, then eventually they are likely to either agree to give in or be tired and distracted enough for a SWAT team to extract them out.

For you this will be more about really understanding what a person is asking for and exposing any falsehoods in their reasoning. If you can do this in a tactful way you can maybe get them to accept another method (your way) of getting to where they want to be and to changing their mind in the process. Combining a few of these strategies might look like this;

- "Why would it be important for you to get those specific terms?"

- "How would you envisage it looking if you got them?"

- "I agree, we are also looking for a very similar solution"

- "This is how I think it would be better for both of us to get there"

This line of questioning and reasoning encompasses everything from building rapport, showing good listening skills, acquiring accurate information to responding with empathetic answers. Try laying out these in advance the next time you encounter a negotiation and I assure you that the responses you will get will be much more open, honest and ultimately more beneficial to everyone. It can seem like magic when it's done well.

SUMMARY

Although the topic of negotiation might sound like a complex and daunting one, as we've seen, it's really only about doing two things. Firstly learning the high level negotiation strategies in preparation for these events and then implementing the right behavior patterns in the moment to effectively pull them off. The former takes some study and the latter more experiential practice.

But prior to that, it is always a good idea to see where we have come from in terms of negotiating these things. What conversations and processes that have got us to this point today. It was only 20,000 or so years ago that humans were settling disputes over land, food and possessions with much more primitive methods. Violence was usually the go to conflict resolution strategy of the time. It has been a slow grinding process since then and it wasn't until around the Renaissance era of the 16th century until we really saw the semblance of our modern day critical thinking strategies of negotiation, and that was still due to conflict and war for the most part.

However the technological and rational parts of the last century moved us on even further. Game Theory simulations to fraught off the cold war and industry standard employment and business contract improvements both playing there parts to shape the negotiation discussion once more. Lastly we come to today, a post modern take on persuasion principles where an interconnected and high speed world dominates decision making. Rudimentary box ticking strategies of the past no longer cut it and have moved aside in favor of more human centric tactics that bring empathy building and irrational human behavior into focus.

So having started at the macro level of warring countries and societies, negotiation principles have nowadays descended right down to the intricacies of the human interaction itself. These were the critical conversations I had to deal with on a daily basis myself. You have to start by firstly identifying general and overarching negotiation personality profiles of both yourself and your opponents. Are you more of a factual negotiator who focuses on the facts and figures or do you focus on the empathy building process like a relational negotiator would? Or do you like to feel out the interaction as you go and adapt accordingly in an intuitive style. In reality a combination of the above, a negotiator who embodies all three styles when it suits them best will be the most optimal operator.

Regardless of in which camp you predominantly fall, you need to make sure you know a couple of critical details before entering into any negotiating room. They are simply your ideal offer level and your reserve or walk away terms. I'm not talking about adhering to a strict set of BATNA rules, but something to guide your opening exchanges. If you know what these are and have fully accepted that you will stick to these levels if triggered and in advance, you should find the whole negotiation process will go much more rationally and without disappointment if you do have to walk away. Dealing with somebody else's emotions to smooth the negation process is one thing, but dealing with your own regarding the facts and figures and possible outcomes is quite another. So make sure you are managing your expectations wisely.

So after taking care of the foundational stuff you now have to switch your attention to start building an empathetic environment. To start employing the verbal and non verbal rapport building strategies to eventually ease you into the negotiation talks themselves. You will find that you should have much less friction and resistance to the points you are proposing if you do things this way.

These instances include the big buying and selling moments in life, where that new car or house is on the line. Whether it's a pitching approach such as the Boulwarism method or trail ballooning to anchor your offer at a favorable level or a thought pattern interrupt to get someone off track. You need to be aware of these strategies before entering into the negotiating fray. Similarly you need to be equally prepared for those business and boardroom meetings when thrashing out new contracts or promotion packages are at stake. Whether you are logrolling to curry favor with colleagues or setting an agenda to best suit your objectives, each strategy needs to be carefully thought out with foresight and planning in order to give them the best chance to play out in your favor.

And finally there is one last element that glues all of these strategies together. The thing that ensures these techniques go smoothly and as planned, and that's your physical behavior patterns when executing them in the moment. This will really determine whether you can negotiate your way to a better deal or not. Everything from building situational empathy to mirroring mannerisms, these behavioral cues will be essential to your negotiation success. For me it was as critical as it could get, where operational margin for error was nonexistent.

CONCLUSION

There are moments in life where simple persuasion techniques will do. However there are other times when the stakes are higher, situations that require a more intentional and measured approach. For these instances you need legitimate negotiating skills.

Whether you like it or not you will be engaging in these types of interactions large and small on a daily basis so you might as well sharpen your talking tools and psychological strategies to better prepare yourself for when they do come around. Whether it's buying that new car or selling the house, you don't need me to tell you that it's critical to get the most out transactions such as these.

This is also true of the business and office negotiation situations you will find yourself in. When it comes to negotiating that pay rise or new contract, you need to make sure you are getting the best possible outcome. As I mentioned in the opening remarks to this book, this doesn't mean you have to employ manipulating or deceitful tactics, but rather the clever psychological tricks I have explained to get things moving in your direction.

These techniques can be highly nuanced and counterintuitive at times and will require a fair amount of practice and patience when initially feeling them out, but it will be well worth the effort. I literally have no idea how much more I have gained over the years by getting just a few percentage points more out of the deals I make on a day-to-day basis.

But remember it really is only a game; a game in which the stakes just vary depending on the level you are playing at. But again this doesn't mean one party necessarily misses out, that it's a competition of winner takes all. I've always found the more collaborative approach works best as opposed to a competitive one as my strategies hopefully illustrate. You have to think of a negotiation as more of a non-zero-sum game where both parties can bring their piece to the table and aggregate your gains rather than the typical adversarial style exchange where somebody has to walk away empty handed.

"The best move you can make in negotiation
is to think of an incentive that the other person
hasn't even thought of – and then meet it"

(Eli Broad)

If you enter into these stand-off styles of exchanges, even if you win, you'll more than likely lose out in the long run. You want to avoid creating situations where people feel slighted and can make your life difficult for the next one. Or even worse, out for revenge. You are effectively managing the future within a successful negotiation and not only the momentary value and what is currently on the table. So play the game in good spirit and for the long term, and remember to always be building that situational empathy where ever you can. It's the most valuable currency there is.

So there it is, I have given you the tools and now it's up to you to implement and integrate them into your own life to become the expert negotiator it's truly possible to be.

I wish you the very best of luck!

CPSIA information can be obtained
at www.ICGtesting.com
Printed in the USA
BVHW041656271219
567972BV00011B/165/P